Maestro

Maestro

A SURPRISING STORY ABOUT LEADING BY LISTENING

Roger Nierenberg

Portfolio

PORTFOLIO
Published by the Penguin Group
Penguin Group (USA) Inc., 375 Hudson Street, New York, New York 10014, U.S.A. • Penguin Group (Canada), 90 Eglinton Avenue East, Suite 700, Toronto, Ontario, Canada M4P 2Y3 (a division of Pearson Penguin Canada Inc.) • Penguin Books Ltd, 80 Strand, London WC2R 0RL, England • Penguin Ireland, 25 St. Stephen's Green, Dublin 2, Ireland (a division of Penguin Books Ltd) • Penguin Books Australia Ltd, 250 Camberwell Road, Camberwell, Victoria 3124, Australia (a division of Pearson Australia Group Pty Ltd) • Penguin Books India Pvt Ltd, 11 Community Centre, Panchsheel Park, New Delhi – 110 017, India • Penguin Group (NZ), 67 Apollo Drive, Rosedale, North Shore 0632, New Zealand (a division of Pearson New Zealand Ltd) • Penguin Books (South Africa) (Pty) Ltd, 24 Sturdee Avenue, Rosebank, Johannesburg 2196, South Africa

Penguin Books Ltd, Registered Offices:
80 Strand, London WC2R 0RL, England

First published in 2009 by Portfolio,
a member of Penguin Group (USA) Inc.

10 9 8 7 6 5 4 3 2 1

Copyright © Roger Nierenberg, 2009
All rights reserved

LIBRARY OF CONGRESS CATALOGING IN PUBLICATION DATA

Nierenberg, Roger.
Maestro : a surprising story about leading by listening / Roger Nierenberg.
    p. cm.
Includes index.
ISBN 978–1–59184–288–0
1. Leadership. 2. Listening. 3. Communication. I. Title.
HM1261.N54 2009
303.3'4—dc22   2009022018

Printed in the United States of America
Set in Bembo with Equipoize
Designed by Daniel Lagin

Contents

Getting It All Wrong

MY MEETING WAS BEGINNING TO SPIN OUT OF CONTROL. "For the life of me," cried Sarah in exasperation, "I don't see why we're spending so much time talking about developing this new product when we know that our customers haven't shown any interest in it. We have all the research data. It isn't what they want."

I could see that Rick was about to lose it. "Look out the window, Sarah," he snapped. "Didn't anyone tell you that the economy has changed? Our customers don't know what they want. Your data may seem clear but you're not on the front lines like our salespeople, talking with customers. Look at *our* numbers," he said, shaking the papers in front of him. "They aren't even buying their favorite products the way they used to. Our best shot at staying alive out there is to introduce something new."

"Well"—Sarah's voice dripped sarcasm—"if sales could properly execute the plan with our current products there'd be plenty of results."

I noticed that Malcolm looked eager to join the debate and I called on him to interject. "It's not enough for us to ask what they *want*. We've got to understand what they would rush to buy *if it were offered*."

"Now wait a minute," Mike chimed in. "Let's not throw out

the baby with the bathwater. We've spent a decade developing an incredible production capacity that keeps costs low and quality high. Let's not start switching to expensive new products. In this economy they're not going to buy anything unless it's at an affordable price. Don't forget that."

"Yeah, but are we taking full advantage of the new technologies we can harness?" Ethan countered. "We've come up with some groundbreaking ideas we could develop, if sales and marketing wouldn't always shoot them down."

I'd seen this type of argument break out in meetings before: the heads of marketing, sales, strategy, manufacturing, and R&D going after one another. I had to stop it now because I'd learned that their bickering could degenerate quickly.

"Look, everybody, just calm down. This quarreling is getting us nowhere."

I was already in my second month as the head of this troubled division but I didn't seem to be making any progress with my team. When the CEO recruited me, I was charged with reversing our downward slide, and helping to return the company to profitability. Initially I was excited about the seasoned high-level executives who would form my leadership team.

Large or small, every group I'd led during my twenty-five-year career had outperformed its expectations. Now this was my chance to bring that kind of success to a team of leaders who were the cream of the crop. I felt confident that my group had the talent to bounce back; it was simply suffering from a lack of strong leadership. And I was eager to prove that my division could guide the company to its former heights.

I soon discovered, however, that this team did not act like the ones I'd led before. Despite their skills, these experts had settled into attitudes that were so colored by their diverse professional disciplines that they continually locked horns over whatever issue was up for discussion. For such intelligent people, they were surprisingly blind to any potential common ground between them, or simply unwilling to acknowledge it.

"I'm determined to move forward on this issue," I announced after yet another fruitless product-development meeting. "I'm going to schedule one-on-one meetings this week with each of you. I want to hear all points of view and then we can reach a resolution once and for all."

Throughout my career I'd often found that breaking a problem down into its most basic elements would eventually lead me to its solution. In fact, I've always loved the challenge of bringing order to a collection of interlocking parts, like solving a jigsaw puzzle. Sorting out all those strangely shaped pieces and seeing them fall into place gave me enormous satisfaction. But with a company as large as this one most of the pieces lay beyond my own reach, and I had to enlist my team members to help me put them in order. It was certainly not a one-man job, and I was beginning to doubt whether my team would ever be able to solve this puzzle.

Despite my doubts, the individual meetings with my department heads later that week went very well. I was impressed by how capably each leader managed his unit's day-to-day problems and challenges. I could feel how ambitious they were about exceeding the quarterly performance targets. I learned about their priorities and how they viewed the company's future. After hearing all points of view, I was convinced that I could find their common ground and arrive at the best way for them to work together.

At the next group meeting I thanked them all for offering me such useful feedback, and assured them that I had listened very carefully. Then I announced our new battle plan, and laid out the actions each leader would take in implementing it. Because it was so important that they understand my plan I diagrammed the process in some detail on a chart.

When I finished my explanation the room was silent. I surmised that the presentation had gone over well, because when I asked for questions nobody had any to ask. Success! My team had finally turned a corner, and I was relieved that we were now moving forward with one clear plan.

But during the following weeks my hope again turned to frustration as it gradually dawned on me that each leader was still focusing solely on the success of his own division. There was no more collaboration across units than there had been before. People were working hard, but it was as if they had blinders on. It seemed that despite my best efforts, nothing much had changed.

Then the bombshell hit—a call from the CEO.

"How's it going?" he asked.

"Oh, things are going well. I developed a very good plan and we're implementing it now."

"Well, I hear through the grapevine that your team is not working well together. They're not sensing strong leadership from you and things are a bit adrift. I just thought you'd want to know."

How could that be? I had laid out a plan. I detailed what had to be done and by whom. I drew it all out on the board. They understood it. No one raised any objections. I was shocked. And, even more than the assertion that my team wasn't working well together, the criticism of my leadership stung me. I was doing the same things that had worked with my teams in the past. What was so different now?

Hearing from the CEO was not only embarrassing and distressing, but it was just the latest letdown in two months of intensity and disappointment at work. One of the few bright spots in the day had become my trip to the gym, and that evening's workout was longer than most.

By the time I made it home my sixteen-year-old daughter

was finishing a violin lesson in the living room with her teacher, Robert. As I rummaged through the fridge for leftovers, I overheard him raving about the new conductor of his orchestra. "He's got this rare ability of getting headstrong and independent people like us to set aside our differences and work toward making the music come alive."

Headstrong? Set aside their differences? Boy, did that sound familiar. I was curious to hear about anyone who could get willful and stubborn professionals to collaborate, so I brought it up to Robert as I walked him out to his car.

"I couldn't help but hear what you said about the new conductor of your orchestra. You seem very excited about him."

"I am. Like I was saying to your daughter, we don't know exactly how he does it, but he makes the entire orchestra speak with one voice. Suddenly we're all playing with our full artistry at every performance. When he's on the podium it's as if the differences between us somehow magically disappear, which in turn promotes trust and confidence. "

"Trust in him?" I asked.

He hesitated. "I guess so, but I think we get the feeling that he trusts *us*. Somehow that makes us work together so much better. It never seems as if he's dictating. You always feel like you're contributing toward something bigger than yourself."

Robert was clearly inspired by his new leader, and his description of the effects on the orchestra made me very intrigued. I was looking for any new inspiration to relieve some of the pressure at work. "I'd love to understand how he works," I said.

"Well, why not come to a rehearsal?" Robert proposed. "You could see him in action and draw your own conclusions."

I had no idea what I was going to learn when I decided to sit in on an orchestra rehearsal, but I was certainly willing to give it a try.

From a seat in the concert hall all professional musicians look pretty much alike dressed in tails or long black dresses. But when I walked through the backstage entrance and got a close look at some of the players as they arrived, I saw them for the first time as individuals.

This was, in fact, a far more diverse group than the employees at my company. None of them was formally dressed, but while many looked stylish and trendy, some others even wore sweatpants and T-shirts. The women were shod in anything from high heels to hiking boots. And I noticed some men with close-cropped hair, while others looked so shaggy that heads would have turned at the office.

I heard quite a few foreign languages as I made my way toward the stage. The average age seemed to be about forty, though some looked fresh out of college and others seemed to be in their sixties. Wow, I thought, these people are so different, one from the other. I wondered how the conductor got these people to work together.

At last I saw a familiar face. Robert was waiting for me and he led me onto the stage, where the musicians were unpacking their instruments. "I've arranged everything. It's fine for you to be up here." He pointed to a chair. "There's an extra place set up for you at the back of the viola section. Have fun." And with a friendly wave of his hand he headed toward the violin section to find his own seat.

By now the stage was full, and when a man in the violin section stood up, the orchestra grew quiet. Then, right behind me, the oboe played a long note and everybody started tuning their instruments. Finally the conductor, who had been standing off to the side while the musicians readied themselves, stepped up onto the podium.

"Good morning, ladies and gentlemen," he began. "Let's play the last movement: Allegro vivacissimo."

People started turning the pages on their music stands. When they found the right spot they sat up and raised their instruments. I was watching the conductor, who seemed to be reading the orchestra, waiting for them to be ready. Finally he raised his baton and held it steady. The room was silent. Then he made a quick, sudden, compact movement of the baton and the room burst into sound.

I was stunned by the orchestra's response. It was like a pack of racers reacting to the starting gun. Pow! All the musicians left the starting blocks at exactly the same instant, with not a single one ahead of or behind the others.

And I'd never heard music in this way. In my chair at the back of the viola section I was *inside* the sound; surrounded by instruments of every kind. There were cellos to my left and bassoons and horns behind me. The music was so close to me that there didn't seem to be any difference between hearing with my ears and feeling the vibrations coursing through my body.

I stared at the violas, who were playing a repeated note with such vehemence and punch that it was hard to believe they hadn't all suddenly become quite angry. As I looked around the room I realized that the musicians' expressions and body language were different from one another, some intense and serious, others extroverted and playful. All of this activity and energy seemed to have started with that little motion of the baton. What power!

Eventually the conductor stopped moving the baton and held both hands up. The orchestra gradually ground to a halt, like a train whose brakes have been applied but that takes a while to come to a full stop.

"Thank you," he said as the orchestra had just about quieted down. When there was enough silence for him to be clearly heard he turned to the violins. "Violins, concentrate your bows.

Get the same *forte,* but with less bow. Articulate, articulate!" he said, nodding his head at them to reinforce his message. "And be careful to find the pulse in the horns and bassoons. Your double-dotted quarter notes weren't quite long enough."

I had no idea what he was talking about. But before my mind had time to process this new language, he raised the baton again, and they played. I listened now for the second time. The music sounded so complex, but to my ear it was completely synchronized. So many different instruments coming from every part of the stage, so disciplined and so coordinated.

As the rehearsal proceeded I gradually recognized a pattern: they would play, he would comment, they would play again and fix whatever flaws he'd found. If they didn't, he would make them do it again until it was right. They continued in this way for maybe an hour and a quarter. By then I thought that I'd figured it all out.

The orchestra worked like a mechanical clock. It was composed of a series of interlocking parts that needed to be perfectly synchronized. Just as a clockmaker painstakingly takes great care to eliminate the slightest irregularity that could affect accuracy, so the conductor found any points of friction or misalignment, and reshaped the orchestra's playing to fix it. Like a clockmaker, he had a detailed understanding of how the parts fit together, and was a specialist in regulating the mechanism. That's what all of this talk about note lengths, articulation, balance, and strokes was about.

Just as the clock has a mainspring whose energy is transferred through the mechanism until it ultimately moves the hands at exactly the right speeds, so the baton generates the power that the players convert into sound. It not only provides the energy, but also gives precise directions about the tempo.

Rehearsals seemed to be for the conductor to tell the musicians what to do and not to do, and for them to carry out his instructions. His success came from being demanding, not settling for anything less than his high standards. By making the musicians repeat a passage until it was right he let them know that they couldn't get away with anything less. I could see why Robert was impressed by him. Here was a leader who could isolate the faulty part and refine it until it connected flawlessly with the next piece in the puzzle.

I was pretty proud of myself for having so quickly come to an understanding of how everything worked in the orchestra. Then something unexpected happened. The conductor announced that he wanted to step down and listen to the piece as the audience would hear it. He left the stage and said nothing more. After a few moments, when they could see that he had reached a seat in the hall, the musicians started by themselves, and continued to play with the same synchronicity as before.

To tell the truth, it sounded every bit as good to me. Eventually they came to a passage that I'd begun to recognize, where they had to slow down just a bit and then resume in the original tempo. I was sure that they'd bungle this tricky part. But no, they negotiated the transition just as smoothly as when the conductor had been on the podium. When the music came to the end he called out from the hall, "Break." The musicians immediately began putting their instruments into their cases and the stage was suddenly alive with conversation.

I sat in my chair, now perplexed by what I'd just seen. If the baton was the mainspring, how could they play without it? How did they start without the conductor's signal? How did they stay synchronized, even through the transition, without direction from the podium? I was so puzzled that I had to ask the oboist behind me, who was still at work cleaning his instrument.

"Excuse me, but could I ask you a question?"

"Sure," he said, and laid the oboe on his lap.

"You all played without the conductor just then, right?" He nodded with an expression that suggested this was nothing special.

"Well"—I tried not to sound foolish—"how does that work?"

"We're perfectly capable of doing that."

"But you stayed together. You even started together." He sat waiting for my question. "How can you do that without him?" I said, pointing toward the podium.

He laughed. "We don't really need him for that. Most of that stuff we can do ourselves." At that moment one of his fellow musicians came over to discuss an upcoming orchestra committee meeting. The oboist excused himself and fell into conversation with his friend.

I was really confused now. My assessment of how the orchestra works didn't fit at all with what I'd just seen and heard. How did they so skillfully act as one entity, without any one person to follow? The more I thought about it, the more questions sprang up.

For the rest of the day I kept on trying to figure it out, replaying in my mind various memories from the rehearsal. I wasn't quite sure how it worked, but I definitely knew that my original model was quite wrong. The orchestra wasn't much like a mechanical clock after all and the conductor's baton wasn't anything like a mainspring.

The Numbers Don't Add Up

I SWALLOWED HARD. JIM, THE FINANCE DIRECTOR, HAD just shown me the projections for the next three months. "We'd better not tell the others," I said. "They'll probably start sending their résumés around."

Indeed, if the current trends weren't reversed we'd all be out of a job, starting with me. I was most directly accountable for turning the business around, and no one felt the ramifications of these numbers more strongly than I.

The first step had been to stem the bleeding: keep expenses in check, eliminate waste, cut budgets, reduce staff. In order to manage our bottom line I had tightened my control over the company's operations and finances. And now all major decisions crossed my desk. I needed to know more about what was going on than anyone else. Since many parts of the organization didn't communicate well with one another it was clear that I would need access to all the information. But controlling information and expenses wasn't going to generate any *new* *business*.

"You know what I can't understand about the people here?" I wondered aloud to Jim. "It's the opportunities that they let slip through their hands."

"Like what?" he asked.

"Well, for example, one of our scientists attended an industry convention a while back where some really elite researchers were presenting their latest findings. He meets his college roommate there, and discovers that the guy is working for one of our major competitors. They talk shop, the way scientists do, and he learns that the competitor is using some new technology to develop a brand-new product. And when he returns to the office, do you know what he does with that pearl?"

Jim shrugged his shoulders.

"Nothing!" I said a little too vehemently. I could feel my frustration beginning to rise. "He doesn't tell anyone about it. No, not until their product was announced in the news last week, and then he revealed that he'd known about it for more than six months."

"Why didn't he tell anyone?"

"Exactly my point. He said that he didn't realize anyone would be interested!" I exclaimed in irritation. "But this is not an isolated incident.

"Actually, I've seen that myself," Jim joined in. "One of my own guys went to a financial meeting and heard a competitor making a presentation to investors. He never passed the information on to anyone. When he was confronted about it he got real huffy. He said he was there to make a presentation for the company, not to do its intelligence work."

"This attitude is rampant," I continued. "Salespeople who have a particular expertise will resist introducing their clients to another salesperson with a different specialty, even if it might result in more business for the company. They just don't want to share their commission."

"It seems that people are hoarding clients, hoarding information, even hoarding best practices," Jim concluded.

"People do what they're told, but they don't take any initiative. If an opportunity comes to someone's attention, but it lies astride some company boundary, they won't pursue it." I was shaking my head in bewilderment. "Jim, we've got experienced, intelligent people working here. I keep on pointing out their mistakes, and telling them what to do. But that seems to just make them more passive. I've got to find a way to get this workforce more energized and ambitious for the company."

I looked at my watch and realized that I'd run out of time. I needed to get to the orchestra hall for another rehearsal.

"Well, thanks, Jim, for this report. I'm determined to find a way out of this," I said while I gathered my things. With relief I felt the frustration start to dissipate as my thoughts turned to the orchestra.

Since my first visit I had not been able to get what I'd observed there out of my head. I think the reason it stuck with me was that it offered such a different picture from the one I lived with each day at the office. While change was an urgent priority at my company, in reality it was very hard to quickly make any significant headway. But change in the orchestra was fast, really fast. A few words from the conductor, or a flick of his baton, and the musicians would make adjustments immediately. The changes they made didn't sound forced or seem obedient—the whole process somehow felt organic.

While my daily suggestions and guidance didn't seem to get much traction with my people, the orchestra responded eagerly to the conductor, with alertness and energy. It was captivating to witness and, frankly, it made me jealous. But what stayed with me more than any of this was the way the orchestra, in spite of all its different moving parts, sounded and acted like one integrated unit. I had to know how the conductor was pulling this off.

After that first rehearsal I'd known almost immediately that I wanted to attend another, but next time I didn't want to just sit in. I wanted to talk with the conductor. I wanted him to explain how the relationship worked between him and the musicians. So I had phoned Robert to find out if it was possible. The answer came a few days later, after my daughter's next lesson.

"The maestro says that it will be fine," he had said. "Just show up a few minutes early and go to his dressing room."

Now back at the hall, I knocked on the conductor's dressing room door. "Come in," I heard. So I let myself in and crossed to where he was sitting at an old oak desk. We shook hands as I introduced myself.

"Please, sit down," he said with a friendly smile, gesturing to a worn leather chair across from him. "Had you ever attended an orchestra rehearsal before you came here?"

"Well, I played the clarinet in high school, but that was at a pretty low level. I can't say that I'd ever heard a professional rehearsal before Robert invited me here."

"I certainly hope you enjoyed it. What brings you to see me?"

"Robert is my daughter's violin teacher, and he spoke so highly of your leadership that I became curious to see what you do." I paused for a moment, feeling a little awkward about what I was about to say. "To be honest, I have a feeling that I'm not getting everything that I could out of my people at work. When he invited me to visit the orchestra, I thought to myself, Why not? It would be interesting and I might get some new leadership ideas here. But to be honest, my first visit left me with more questions than answers."

"Well, this will be a new experience for me," he said with a touch of amusement. "I've never had a conversation about leadership with a business executive before. It could be very interesting."

But before he could say any more we heard the oboe sounding the tuning note, and the conductor gestured that it was time to go next door to the rehearsal. "Let's talk about this later," he said as he opened the door. I saw the bright lights of the stage, and heard that classic sound of an orchestra tuning up. I found my chair near the back of the viola section.

Own the Music

"GOOD MORNING, LADIES AND GENTLEMEN," HE SAID. "Let's play the opening."

The conductor waited for a few moments as the musicians readied themselves. When the room became quiet he raised his baton and allowed the concentration to build. The atmosphere was quite still now. Then, with a soft, simple gesture from his right arm, the room filled with a sad and stately music. The silence had been broken, but not the stillness. Everything seemed to be moving in slow motion. The violists' bows all around me appeared to float gently over the strings.

Then, suddenly, I felt a new and deep vibration in my chair. I was looking around the room to see what could have caused it when I realized that the double basses had just begun to play a low, resonant note. Strange, I thought, I felt that sound almost before I heard it.

Next, across the stage, I heard all the violins begin to play, in that same mournful, solemn mood. From my vantage point I could see them all, and by watching their bows move in unison I realized that they were all playing the same music. A few of them were looking up at the conductor, but the majority had their eyes firmly planted on their music stands.

It was quite some time before the conductor signaled the

orchestra to stop. "Let's turn to the opening passage again," he said. "Now, violas, what if you blend your sound with the woodwinds? Try to match their color." They began again and played for a few moments before he stopped them. "Beautiful. Now let the entire orchestra's sound form around the oboe. We all follow him—every nuance."

Again they played, but this time I could swear that I actually felt the musicians concentrating more intensely. But the conductor soon stopped them once again. Speaking to the oboist now, he said, "Why not take a bit more liberty? What if the first note came from silence, without any audible beginning? Everyone will be waiting for your sound, so no need to hurry the attack."

And then, yes, I heard the difference. The music seemed to come from nowhere, and I couldn't even exactly tell when it had begun, as if it had appeared out of a haze. It wasn't only sad or solemn now; it had somehow taken on a shadowy, or even ghostly aura. I can't say why, but that moment filled me with a delicious quiver.

The conductor seemed to be very particular about all kinds of subtle distinctions as he led the musicians, using words such as *intonation, phrasing, dynamics,* and *articulation.* Though I didn't understand exactly what his directions meant, I had no trouble feeling and hearing their effect. Each time he asked for something, the sound of the orchestra would change. The body language of the musicians had also become more fluid as they played. The way they took in the conductor's comments and translated them into action was so immediate.

Throughout the rehearsal I was struck by how this session differed from my expectations. Perhaps I'd seen too many movies, but my image of a conductor had been of a temperamental figure dictating to the musicians and even yelling at them to do what he wanted. This rehearsal was nothing like that. It was collegial and cooperative. While the maestro's words were unambiguous, definite, and confident, his demeanor was open, attentive, and perfectly natural. Again I was awed at how the orchestra responded to him with such alertness. How on earth did he generate such immediate and total cooperation?

When the rehearsal was over the musicians dispersed pretty quickly, and I made my way back through the chairs to the conductor's dressing room. I very much wanted to talk to him about what I had seen.

"Thank you, again, for allowing me to be here," I began. "That was a fascinating experience."

"Did you like the opening of Mendelssohn's *Scottish* Symphony?"

"It has an amazing atmosphere," I responded slowly, searching for the right words to describe such evocative music.

"That's just what we were aiming for. You know, Mendelssohn composed this symphony after his visit to Scotland, which was considered a pretty exotic place then. He sketched the opening passage, which we were rehearsing, after a visit to Holyrood Palace, where Mary, Queen of Scots, had lived centuries earlier. We know that because Mendelssohn wrote a letter about the moment when he found the inspiration for this passage.

"By the time of his visit, the adjoining chapel was an overgrown ruin, everything broken, moldering, and covered in ivy. I'm convinced that the vision for this passage must have appeared as if from the distant past, clouded in mystery and solemnity. Reading his letter helped me to imagine the right sound for this passage, and that's what we were working so hard to find today."

"What stunned me was how quickly they responded to you and worked with you to get that effect. How did you get them to do that?"

It may have sounded like a compliment to him, but this question was actually gnawing at me. My admiration for the conductor's impact on the orchestra was mixed with considerable envy.

"They've become a very flexible group."

"But how did you achieve that? Robert said that it wasn't this way until you came."

"Well, that's very kind of him." He pursed his lips, reflecting on my question.

"I guess I would start by saying that it doesn't work too well to order musicians to be responsive or cooperative," he began. "At the beginning of my career, like many young conductors, I thought my role was to tell the orchestra how to play, and theirs was to carry out my directions. Eventually I couldn't help noticing how lackluster the orchestra's response was. Rehearsals felt tedious and difficult; performances sounded competent at best, and often really quite dull. I was certainly putting out, but my own inspiration never seemed to reach the players. If it did, they didn't seem to want to be part of it.

"Eventually I realized that a great performance would happen only when the motivation sprang as much from them as from me. I learned to see my job as simply creating an environment where that could happen. Once I learned to engage their artistry, everything felt so much easier."

I could feel myself get tense as I listened to this response. I was a long way from getting my people energized on their own. "But how did you get them to feel that way?" I asked.

"By acknowledging that they own the music as much as I do."

"What do you mean by 'own the music'?"

"Let me explain it this way. Each musician reads the part on his own stand, which, in effect, tells him his assignment: 'Play these notes.' It's very easy for the musician to let the part define his responsibility, to draw boundaries around it, to separate his job from what others do. But we know that music is an intensely collaborative art. Every musician must adjust his playing to what everyone else is doing: tune to them, balance to them, match their sound and articulation, et cetera. Now take this same musician and put him in a solo recital, and he will feel complete ownership of not only his part, but the entire piece. The lion's share of the musical decisions will be in his hands."

"Musical decisions?"

"Artistic decisions, like tempo, mood, phrasing, pacing—whatever is required to turn pages of notes into a live, breathing performance. When he feels in control he will surely take ownership. Put the same musician in an orchestra with seventy-five other musicians, and there is no way that those artistic decisions can be made collectively. Those decisions become the job of the conductor, who doesn't actually make a sound, but has to direct the whole operation."

"That's the classic executive function," I said. "We don't do the work ourselves, but direct others who do."

"Yes, but there's a pitfall that I try very hard to avoid. Can you see it?"

I shook my head.

"You see, it's easy for the musicians to feel as if they are serving the conductor. They even call their rehearsals and performances 'services.' The very physical structure of the organization—with the orchestra radiating out from a central raised platform and the conductor standing over them—promotes that dynamic. In this kind of an environment, many orchestral musicians feel disconnected."

"Yes," I said, nodding. "It's a perfect setup for 'Shut up and do what you're told.'"

"Exactly. The very context of an orchestra fosters a culture in which the players don't own the work; the conductor does."

"I think many large organizations work that way," I added, "and probably even many small ones. But you said that you're dedicated to avoiding this pitfall. How do you do it?" I felt like I'd come back to my original question.

"If a leader wants his people to truly own the work, then he has to be willing to let go of some control. A conductor can't control a big group the way a solo musician controls his instrument. Striving for that kind of direct control will lead him right into this trap."

This was a very challenging notion for me. At the office I was working as hard as I could to control our spending, make sure that income targets were met, resolve seemingly endless debates, make sure that deadlines were observed. I couldn't just give up direct control, as he appeared to be advocating.

"I don't think you really mean what you're saying," I insisted. "Your orchestra seemed to be *totally* under your control today. Frankly, I've never seen such a willingness to contribute."

"I think that willingness is evidence that they make the choice themselves. You can force compliance with your directions, you can require obedience, but you can't mandate enthusiasm, creativity, fresh thinking, or inspiration. If you value that, then people need to feel ownership of the work, and the leader must cede some control to them."

I thought about what I'd seen at the rehearsal. "I noticed that at one point you had the orchestra follow the oboe. Is that an example of what you mean?"

"Yes, that's certainly part of it. I could have given a specific direction about how everyone should play the phrase. But by putting the oboist in charge after offering him a few suggestions, the orchestra was able to achieve a kind of unity of sound that simply following orders could never have accomplished. You see, everything I do is aimed at creating a feeling of community and shared responsibility."

I thought about the office. "But is that really *leading*? Aren't you abdicating your responsibility?" His ideas just didn't make any sense to me. How can you cede control when your own neck is on the line?

"Yes, a leader needs to give corrections and directions," he began. "You saw me doing plenty of that during the rehearsal. That is an important part of a conductor's job. But there is a more fundamental and crucial driver that was probably not as immediately visible today." He looked directly at me and said, "The most important thing a conductor brings to the orchestra is a vision of the music that the musicians will want to bring to life with their playing."

"What does that mean, 'a vision of the music'?"

"When I step onto the podium my every action should provide answers to questions such as Where are we going? What's the goal? What are our priorities? How do we create a compelling and powerful performance of this piece? What's our plan for getting there? And, very important, Exactly what do the musicians need to do to contribute to that? It is no easy matter to answer these questions at all, much less through your actions.

"You see," the conductor continued, "a strong vision can lead people away from focusing on their part alone toward being aware of the whole. The vision should be lofty enough to stir and challenge people. If it's too limited, then people will feel underutilized and uninspired. But when the musicians take hold of a vision then they attach their playing to it. Tasks that might have previously seemed routine now acquire meaning and beauty. While they are doing their jobs, they're always thinking of the grand vision."

"That's just like that famous story," I broke in, "about the custodian who was mopping the floors at a NASA office during the 1960s. When asked, 'What are you doing?' he replied, 'I'm putting a man on the moon.'"

"Yes. If I can persuade an orchestra to embrace a vision like that, it will do more to align and coordinate them than any direct control I could ever impose."

I was convinced that this had happened today, but I was still puzzled about how it worked.

"I'm confused about this. You said that Mendelssohn's letter had helped you to develop a vision for the right sound, and that's what you were working toward during the rehearsal. But I didn't hear you say a word about that to the orchestra. How did *they* pick up on it?"

"A good question. Reading the letter inspired *me* and helped me to imagine this very special sound—as if the music were emerging from a bygone time. But telling the orchestra about it would probably only confuse the issue, suggesting a different sound image to each musician.

"So I came to the rehearsal with an image already in my mind of the most beautiful way the music can sound. It may seem funny to say, but I *believe* in this image; I feel invested in it. I want to see it made real, and the orchestra is the only way that can happen. Then when I start conducting I listen very carefully to their playing."

His words corresponded with what I had seen as I watched him begin the rehearsal.

"However—and here's the complicated part," he went on. "As I listen, I am also inwardly hearing the imaginary sound that I dreamed up before the rehearsal. Hearing the two versions of the piece superimposed, one real and the other imagined, I find the difference between the two. There's a gap between them, and the work of the rehearsal process is to eliminate that gap."

Suddenly it clicked. "That's just like a gap analysis!"

He looked so nonplussed by my words that I had to quickly stifle my amusement. During the entire rehearsal I had been bewildered by the many technical musical terms I'd heard. Now it was my turn to explain some jargon to him.

"A gap analysis is a technique for determining the difference between what is deemed to be possible and what the actual results are. That's the gap. And that gap is what you try to close, or even eliminate."

"Well, yes," the conductor replied. "That's more or less what I'm doing in the rehearsal, trying to close the gap. Of course, much of what I hear is very good, and it's critically important to appreciate that."

"Why? Aren't you focused on executing your vision and how they need to change to make it happen?"

"Yes . . ." He hesitated, thinking about what I had said. "But I want the musicians to feel encouraged to offer all that they have, *even if I haven't thought of it myself.* If they see that I am listening to them with great interest and curiosity they will feel encouraged to offer more. But if they see that I am too preoccupied with my own concerns to really hear them, or worse, that my first reaction is to judge or criticize, they can't help but shut down some part of their talent, and revert to a more defensive mode."

His words made me wonder about what I was offering my people. Sure, I was plenty busy resolving disputes, keeping the company operating, looking after the bottom line. But how much of my energy was going toward encouraging my team, much less conceiving a vision for our future?

The conductor said that a powerful and compelling vision helps people connect their part to the whole. Yet my people's spark seemed to be extinguished every time they came to a boundary within the company. His words almost suggested that my style of leadership played a role in their behavior.

The conductor said that the key to energizing an orchestra's response is inspiring the same vision in all the players. Was that true of my people, or did their visions clash? So often in resolving tedious disputes I resorted to laying down the law. That certainly felt like saying '*do what you're told.*' Was I stumbling into the pitfall the conductor so deliberately sought to avoid?

I realized that this visit with the conductor had sparked more useful insights in an hour than my last ten years as an executive. So, thinking quickly, I decided to make a proposition.

"Would you be interested in doing this again, on a regular basis?

The conductor raised his eyebrows, and took a few seconds to think it over. "Why don't you come and watch us rehearse twice a month. Then afterward we can meet like we did today."

As I drove home I couldn't get the music I'd heard out of my ear. It seemed that my proximity to the players had drilled their sound deeper into my consciousness than I'd remembered music ever penetrating. It was clear to me that more conversations with the conductor could be very useful.

Stuck in a Rut

THE NUMBERS WERE IN. WE HAD NOW MISSED OUR TAR-gets for the second straight month. When I asked the sales team what we were going to do about this they brought me reports filled with data showing that all our products had suffered considerable drops, and dissecting the falloff through all kinds of metrics.

I was frustrated. This was like putting a magnifying glass to the rearview mirror. All of this data about past performance alone wouldn't help us to forge a strategy for success. So I challenged Rick and his sales force to come up with an innovative solution to our lagging sales. "Find me the tools for climbing out of this morass!" I grunted.

Rick's team stared at me blankly. It was becoming painfully clear to me that our company had enjoyed such sustained success, we had forgotten how to innovate. If my best and brightest were struggling to deliver useful insights about how to improve, I knew our future was grim.

So I decided to take the initiative and scheduled meetings with a number of our most important clients. I wanted to hear with my own ears about their difficulties and new anxieties. I didn't go into these meetings with the intention of selling. Instead, I asked probing questions, imploring them to level with me about why their buying patterns had changed. I learned that they were struggling just as much as we were, and simply couldn't buy in the same quantities they used to.

I asked more questions and in the process discovered an opportunity for us. In order to survive, our customers needed some new types of products and services, many that neither we nor our competitors were offering. If we acted quickly, we could easily be the first to provide fresh solutions for their newfound needs.

At my next group meeting with the heads of each major division I explained my revelation and unveiled a program to provide new products and services that were in line with what our customers needed *now*. I demonstrated how each branch of the organization would contribute and gave exact directions about how each should proceed.

I remembered what the maestro had told me about getting the musicians to own the music. But for this brand new initiative I thought it would help my people to give them some more detailed information. At the end of the meeting I was satisfied that everyone walked out of the room knowing what hurdles they would face and exactly what they should do to clear them.

Afterward I congratulated myself on what I considered a particularly successful meeting. I had offered my team an inspiring vision, one that would certainly challenge them.

However, in the coming weeks I saw that the salespeople might be carrying out my directions to the letter, but they had completely missed the spirit. For all their activity in those weeks, we still knew nothing more about our customers' evolving needs than we did at the first meeting.

"Did you guys follow up with customers after my visit?" I asked Rick.

"Yes."

"Then why don't we have any new insights about their concerns?"

"When my people met with the customers they felt very awkward about not being able to immediately provide solutions to their new problems," he explained. "This process was new to us. It wasn't exactly like selling. The sales force is trained to offer answers, decisively and confidently. Since they didn't have any prepared they thought that they'd better get more guidance from you before taking further action."

I was confounded. I had told them exactly what to do and how to do it. Why did such experienced and gifted people need to wait for me to give them directions? Clearly they understood the urgency. Why were they so tentative?

Hear the Clarinet

BEFORE I KNEW IT I WAS ONCE AGAIN SITTING IN THE viola section eagerly waiting for rehearsal to begin. The maestro's manner with the orchestra was professional, as usual. He greeted the musicians and then directed their attention to the passage he intended to rehearse. No superfluous words were spoken and no time was wasted.

I watched him intently as he led the orchestra through the music. The movements of his baton were small and subtle. He was listening intently as his gaze slowly moved around the room, taking in the playing through both his ears and eyes. The orchestra sounded quite good to me, and I was curious to see what kinds of changes he would bring about—what gap he would try to close.

When he stopped the musicians, he said, "Look at how Mendelssohn scored this passage: the melody in the first violins, and the accompaniment in the seconds and lower strings. Of course, that's what we'd expect. But then he doubles the melody an octave lower in the clarinet. I couldn't hear that."

They began again, and instantly the music sounded more hushed and mysterious. Of course the notes were the same, but now everyone seemed to share the same focus: hearing that hidden clarinet part. After a few moments he stopped them.

Addressing the strings, he asked, "Do you notice how neatly the clarinet plays the rhythm? Let's all do it that way." He turned now to the clarinet. "Don't play out to the strings—make them listen to you."

Then the conductor surprised me as he looked back to the strings and said, "Once we've started please let's not bother looking at the baton; the clarinet is the focus." This was astonishing to me: the conductor was telling the musicians *not* to follow his baton.

When they played the passage again it was remarkable. The music was both still and restless at the same time, like the calm before a storm. After a minute or two the music gathered intensity until it broke out into a violent and sustained outburst, like a tempest. It amazed me how he had shaped the execution and the sound of the whole passage, just by drawing the orchestra's attention to the clarinet.

Next the conductor began to refine the music of the storm. Speaking to the brass and kettledrums, he said, "Very exciting. But it's still more beautiful when it's both powerful and transparent, so the listener can hear a kind of X-ray of every element in this texture. Yes, powerful, but let the woodwinds and strings be heard."

I expected the result to be a weaker sound, but instead the swirling activity of the strings was more audible, and added so much to the overall effect. What was particularly startling to me throughout this process was that the differences were so readily apparent, even to my untrained ear.

When it was time for the orchestra to take a break I lingered on the stage as most of the musicians were making their way to the lounge. Nearby I overheard a conversation. "That was ingenious," a violinist was saying to her stand partner as she was laying her violin in its case. "The way he asked us to listen to the clarinet! As many times as I've played that piece, no conductor has ever asked for that." Her colleague was nodding in agreement.

I was intrigued by their reaction and walked over to see if they would tell me more.

"I was curious myself," I remarked, "about the way he rehearsed that passage. What made his approach so different?"

"Well," began one of the violinists, "most conductors seem satisfied with whatever we offer the first time."

"Yes," interrupted her colleague, "and those that do choose to rehearse it just shush us up, which is annoying, and makes us get tense."

"I'm not sure I see the difference," I said. "What he did today created a hushed sound, didn't it?"

"Yes, but by listening to the clarinet we found that sound ourselves, and that somehow made it so much easier."

"And then," the other went on, "it's tricky and awkward to play both very quietly and with good rhythm. But when we imitated the clarinet we all found a way of doing both. It felt so simple."

"And also, it inspired us," said the first.

"How so?" I asked.

"Because it gave us more respect for Mendelssohn—this beautiful little detail that we'd never noticed before: that low clarinet part."

Now I was really eager to talk with the conductor. As soon as the rehearsal was over I made my way once again to his dressing room. Today he was expecting me, and invited me in.

"I noticed that during the rehearsal you seemed to avoid telling the musicians what you wanted them to do. Instead, you often directed their attention toward a particular instrument, like that quiet clarinet part. Was that deliberate?"

"That's quite right," he said, smiling with slight embarrassment, as if one of his secrets had been discovered. "What else did you notice?"

I tried to remember the details of the rehearsal. "You rarely asked the orchestra to focus on something *you* were doing. In fact, at one point you told the orchestra *not* to watch your baton."

"Yes, you're really on to something here." He invited me to sit down, as if to suggest that this would not be a short discussion. "When I was a young conductor I did think that the best way to help the orchestra was to tell them what to do. I used my direct channel of communication with each individual musician to convey instructions, either verbally or through the movements of my baton. You might call this the hub-and-spoke approach."

"So if you were using that approach today in that passage, you would have gone directly to the problem, and just told the strings to play softer?" I suggested. That's what I'd always thought leaders *should* do.

"Exactly," he pronounced with emphasis, "that's hub-and-spoke. Now, if your directions are both clear and correct, you *can* get results this way. But the orchestra's talent and energy will be eroded. They will never play to their highest level."

"Why is that, if the directions are correct?"

"Because such a conductor places his influence between the musicians and their engagement with the music."

This was baffling for me. Why beat around the bush? Just tell your people when something needs to be corrected and hold them accountable for doing it. "I'm sorry, but I really don't see what's wrong with giving correct directions."

He weighed his answer carefully. "Yes, it's a subtle distinction, but a crucial one. When you step onto the podium you assume all the authority that comes with it. You can use that authority to appoint yourself as the fountainhead—the sole source of all judgment and feedback. In that model, if it's too loud you'll just tell them so.

"But there are two problems with that style of leadership. First, by making your feedback supreme you are actually sending the message that the players should suspend their judgment until you've ruled on what should be done. You are using the power of the podium to actually render your people more passive."

"That's the pitfall, isn't it?"

"Yes, the pitfall that undermines their ownership of the work. Second, your feedback doesn't come in real time. You have to stop the orchestra and then tell the musicians. The delay between their action and your feedback invites potential confusion or misunderstanding. Exactly when was it too loud? All the time? Was it ever okay? How soft is soft enough? Their only way to answer these questions is to wait until you've made your pronouncement. But you will never have enough time to talk about everything. There will always be some areas of ambiguity."

I shook my head knowingly as he spoke. This scenario sounded all too familiar. Then I thought about my conversation with the two violinists. I now understood their irritation toward conductors who "shushed them up." They would find out what was right or wrong only after the fact, and even then with a degree of vagueness. I saw how this could dull their ability and their willingness to make the necessary adjustments on their own.

"So what do you do? Just let it be too loud?"

"No, no," he said with a smile, "there is a far more effective way to get results, and it's easier for both the leader and the players. Once again it starts with the leader being willing to cede some control to the musicians. You acknowledge that they are artists too, with a highly developed capacity for making musical judgments. So from your podium you identify a focal point for the orchestra to zoom in on."

"Like the clarinet," I suggested.

"Right. I chose the clarinet because it's very soft and hidden. In order to hear it you have to play very quietly. Now the musicians are no longer looking to the conductor for feedback. They are using *their own ears*. And I ask them *not* to watch the baton because I don't want any distraction from their focus on listening. They are now taking in the feedback—detailed, real-time feedback—and mobilizing all of their talent to do so."

Whew! This was a big idea. I was struggling a bit to get my mind around it. "But then you're not telling them whether it's too loud. What if they don't understand the point you want to make or misinterpret your meaning? Aren't you really abdicating your leadership role?"

"This is a different kind of leadership. It is my responsibility to understand the structure of the music and the roles within the orchestra well enough to choose the right focus. I invite the musicians to hear it, and let their ears do the work of finding how soft their playing needs to be. They have good ears, you know, and can do it far better without my intervening. You see, the musicians definitely do feel a certain link to the conductor, but it will never be as strong as their connection to the *sounds* they're making, and to the other musicians' sounds. A wise leader will leverage that, and use it to direct the orchestra toward making the vision happen."

The very first time I sat inside the orchestra I had been convinced that it was like a clock, and the conductor was a kind of repairman who would fix the parts. But now I had observed that it was no machine at all, but a living thing that had awareness, intelligence, and judgment. It had its own collective artistry and knowledge base, too.

I was beginning to see that there was a way to lead people that focused their own energy and directed it—a leadership that didn't open the clock and repair a faulty part. Instead the leader's role was to focus the group's consciousness on a point of the highest leverage, where a small adjustment could bring about rapid and organic change.

I remembered that Buckminster Fuller, the famous futurist, had often compared himself to a trim tab, the small rudder that's attached to the main rudder of a ship. A large rudder can be extremely difficult to turn because it must move an enormous volume of water. The trim tab is tiny by comparison, yet when it moves it brings the larger rudder along, which turns the massive ship. The proper leverage point can bring about large-scale change without a huge amount of effort. I saw today that the conductor's art was in choosing the right leverage point to make the whole system react and move in the desired direction.

"How do you know what they should focus on?" I asked after a long pause.

"There's a real art to that," he replied thoughtfully. "When you study the score, you look for the interrelationship of the parts and the whole, to find the key that effortlessly opens the door. Sometimes listening for the instruments that have the fastest notes snaps everything into place. Sometimes assigning specific roles blends the orchestra's sound: distinguishing who leads and who supports. Sometimes clarifying foreground, middle ground, and background is what they need."

I was still shaking my head at what I was hearing. "And just listening for these things will actually solve the problem faster than giving corrections?"

"Often faster, and always better. Of course, a very foolish conductor will do the opposite: reduce the musicians to behaving like robots, by demanding that they suspend their own judgment and submit to his. But with the right leadership there is a special feeling that blossoms in an orchestra when it is really absorbed and fascinated by its own sound. Things become transparent, and no matter where they're sitting, the musicians can hear the whole orchestra. They feel free to engage their artistry and become less dependent on the conductor. Every orchestra loves this feeling, yet the musicians themselves are almost helpless to cause it to happen. Only the conductor can."

"So that was what you had in mind when you spoke to the brass and kettledrums about an X-ray of the orchestra."

"Right. And when you have made transparency and listening a high priority and found ways to engage your musicians in it, then the orchestra magically transforms itself into a community. That is, in fact, the basis for everything that I do. Every word that I speak, every inflection in my tone of voice, every gesture is directed toward the goal of creating a feeling of community. A community simply acts faster, more intelligently, more creatively, and with more joy than a group that is primarily focused on its leader. The hub-and-spoke approach drains the life out of a living system."

I left the hall that day with very mixed feelings. Much of what the conductor said ran counter to what I'd always believed and practiced. I was wishing that I could find a way to dismiss him or find loopholes in his methods. After all, what did he know about business? He worked only with notes. Leading an orchestra was about as far from my world of strategic management, budgeting, and allocating resources as you could get.

Yet I found it extremely difficult to dismiss him. There were the results I'd seen and heard—the energy, the unity, the speed, the flexibility, and yes, the sense of community. And then there was that amazing, unforgettable difference in the sound when the orchestra listened to the clarinet. How seemingly effortless it was for the entire group to achieve such subtlety. All because the conductor discovered the right trim tab and drew the players' attention to it.

So why couldn't I do the same? Couldn't there be a way to focus the sales force's attention directly on the customer's voice, the way the orchestra listened for the clarinet? In the same way that the conductor told the musicians not to watch the baton, maybe I should wean my people off their reliance on me to translate the customer's needs. Then, wouldn't our reactions be faster and more accurate? Wouldn't my people grow in confidence, knowing that I was trusting their judgment to understand and react to what they were hearing? Was it in my power to replace my hub-and-spoke leadership with a more community-oriented approach?

These questions shook the foundations of a leadership approach that I thought had been working well for me for so long. But when the memory of the orchestra's playing came back to me I realized that it was the sound that gave validation to his ideas. If I needed any proof that this kind of change was possible, I had heard it with my own ears.

So I decided to put this new kind of leadership to the test. The next day I would let my sales reps know that I needed them to start coming up with some new ideas without my help. I understood that listening to our clients' problems without having ready solutions felt awkward and foreign to them, but they needed to get into the habit of making that kind of conversation a part of every client meeting.

I would challenge them to ask their contacts about how our existing products were lacking and even what changes they thought we could make to be more aligned with the changes in their business. And I would urge them to listen attentively for what the client might be thinking but had not yet said. My reps could then present to me what they'd learned along with suggestions about what new products and services we should consider developing to meet these needs, or what modifications we could make to our existing lines.

That plan didn't seem so radical, but I had my doubts that I could let my people take their own path to finding the innovative results we so desperately needed. I felt as uncomfortable as they would be—but maybe that was a good thing.

A Stalemate

WHEN WE GAVE HIGHEST PRIORITY TO CLEARLY AND AC-
curately hearing the customer's voice, it made a big difference
in figuring out how to turn around our weak sales figures. The
challenge I posed to my sales reps was—to my amazement—
already beginning to yield some encouraging results.

So I decided to start meeting with and listening more carefully to our key suppliers, too. Not surprisingly, many of them
confessed to having cash-flow problems. And worse, they were
exasperated with us because of our chronically late payments.

Improving our relationship with important suppliers was a
vital element in my strategy, so I sent out a directive to Ted, the
chief accountant, ordering that, within a month's time, our
time frame for processing payments should be shortened by 25
percent.

At the end of the next month I measured our progress in our
monthly performance data. I knew that a 25 percent improvement
might not be possible in the first month but it was pretty upsetting
to see that the payment cycle was absolutely unchanged.

"Find out what happened," I ordered Ted.

"Okay, but you do realize that it is an extremely difficult
matter to shorten the time it takes to process these payments."

"How can that be?" I asked with some irritation. "Why can't

they just get it done? Are the people at accounts payable simpletons?

Two weeks later he reported back to me.

"Sir, in my opinion the folks down in accounts payable are quite expert," Ted declared. "They've created a system for processing invoices that's extremely accurate, reliable, and fast. I was very impressed by the care they'd taken in designing and implementing it. The employees are very conscientious."

"Then why the delays?"

"You see," he said glumly, "it's the interface with purchasing."

I must have grimaced pretty obviously because he quickly came to the purchasing department's defense.

"The problem is not with the *people* at purchasing. It's that their information system doesn't communicate easily with accounts payable's."

He saw me raise my finger, so he continued before I could interrupt.

"Now, accounts payable has been extremely clever in devising all kinds of work-arounds. They do process the information from purchasing, of course. But they frequently have to call or e-mail for clarification about vendor numbers or product labels. And that's the moment in the process where errors creep in. Errors that slow things down even more."

"Didn't accounts payable ever ask purchasing to change their formatting?"

"Yes, of course, many times, and vice versa. But there's no love lost between the two departments. Each sees the other as the source of the problem, and each is a bit puffed up about the virtues of its own system."

"So they're stalemated?"

"Yes, I'm afraid so. Both departments have simply accepted the frustrations of their situation. They can't see a way to make it better, so they point fingers at each other."

Tell the Whole Story

THE CONDUCTOR'S IDEAS ABOUT LEADERSHIP WERE STILL very present in my mind since our last visit. They had turned my conception of what it means to be a leader on its head. And even though I had already seen signs of growth after putting his methods to the test on my own team, I was still a bit leery to discover how our next meeting would challenge my beliefs.

But however hesitant I might have felt about hearing some of his ideas, I had committed to these next few visits with the maestro. And, in any case, I couldn't deny the draw of the rehearsals themselves. Being inside all of that sound energized me in a way I'd never quite felt before. At home, and even at the office, I'd notice that this music was playing inside my head as I went about my day. It was becoming a kind of companion.

I walked onto the stage and found my accustomed place in the viola section, nodded a greeting to the players around me, who by now had gotten used to my being here. Then as usual the orchestra tuned and the conductor stepped onto the podium. "Adagio," was all he said, and the musicians turned their pages until they were ready.

The first thing I noticed when they began to play was that the violinists had all put their bows in their laps and were plucking their instruments instead. I looked over to the second violins, and they were doing the same. Then the first violins began a sweet melody that seemed to float lightly through the hall. It looked like they were really pouring their hearts out and it struck me that they were playing a kind of love song.

Eventually the violin part gave way to what sounded like a dignified slow procession played by the winds. It began quietly, but continually grew in strength until the kettledrum joined in at the climax. Then the violin tune resumed.

Finally the conductor stopped the orchestra.

"First violins, bravo. Think a longer phrase. Tell the whole story of the melody, not just the first four bars. It's twenty measures long, you know, and the high note doesn't come until the fourteenth bar of the tune. Make a long, arcing line. Don't make so much out of each nuance."

As usual, this meant nothing to me, but clearly the violinists understood, because a few of them were nodding their heads in agreement.

"Seconds and violas, shape your accompaniment to the melody." Then they played.

Throughout the rehearsal the conductor seemed to be talking a lot about flow. He constantly pointed out where the "goal of the phrase" was, and asked the orchestra not to "break the line." Though I might not have understood his exact directions, they did seem to be making a difference, as I found myself being increasingly swept up in the music. The more he said to the orchestra, the more it seemed like the music was actually in motion. I felt lifted and carried by the sound. It was a very agreeable feeling.

After the rehearsal, when we sat down in his dressing room, I was ready with my first question. "Today you seemed to be focusing a lot on flow. For such a small detail, weren't you emphasizing that a lot?"

"Well, flow may be very basic to music, but that doesn't mean it's a detail, or that it's easy to achieve. It involves far more than just playing the notes correctly. And it directly affects the energy that the musicians feel, the ease with which they can unify, and the degree to which their artistry and imagination can be engaged."

"All of that because of flow?"

"Yes, that and much more. You're quite right to have picked up on it, because it's one of our highest priorities. You see, flow is the bridge that links the present moment to the next. It's the conduit that transfers energy all around the stage and out to the audience." He gave me a telling look. "It's our primary means of creating a sense of community in the orchestra."

"How does the flow of the music create community?"

One of the things I admired about the conductor was that he always took my questions seriously. He was really thinking, and didn't answer me right away. "Okay," he finally said, "have you ever seen one of those games when schoolchildren sit in a circle and pass around an object such as a beanbag?"

I knew exactly what he meant, and I told him about a conference when a troupe of drummers led us in a team-building game in which we passed rocks around.

"Yes, exactly, I've seen the rock game," he said. "Everyone starts with two rocks on the floor in front of them. There's a four-step process. One, you pick up the rocks. Two, you click them together. Three, you place them in front of the person on your left. Four, you clap your hands. Then you pick up two new rocks and begin again. You do all of this in a rhythmic way, so that a steady pulse is generated. The rocks move around the circle in a clockwise direction. It takes some coordination. The laughter comes when things inevitably break down, as people go at different speeds or can't create a steady pulse. Once the flow is broken, rocks will start to pile up in front of one person who can't possibly manage to get rid of them, leaving the next person with no rocks at all."

"Yes, that's exactly what happened," I said, smiling to myself at the memory of that exercise.

"Now, every once in a while, with the right players, something very special happens. A rhythm develops and the players no longer feel like their actions are the source of the pulse, but rather the pulse is the source of their actions. The circle becomes more than a collection of individuals, and through the unity of the pulse it turns into a seamlessly integrated team. Suddenly, what was tricky becomes easy. No one is making any mistakes. The movement of the rocks has turned into a smooth, steady flow. And if you've ever had this experience you'll know that the passage of time itself actually feels different. That is *flow,* and it generates the most delicious feeling of community.

"When you start the game, each person is very conscious of his own movements. But as the group finds its flow, you feel more connected to what everyone else is doing. You're not working in isolation anymore—you're riding on a wave of energy that makes it so much easier to carry out your own task. Your attention is no longer on just your own job, but equally on that of somebody across the circle. You feel just as connected to the rocks that are approaching you as the ones that are in your own hands."

"So that's what you meant when you said that flow connects the present to the future," I said.

"Yes. Flow enables you to actually feel like your consciousness has expanded to include a longer stretch of time. That's why time feels so different at those moments. Your awareness isn't limited to your own movements; it expands to include the whole process."

I could picture what he meant, but didn't see why this was

important. "Okay, so how would you relate this to an orchestra?"

"Well, that intense feeling of unity is what we strive for in an orchestra, but there are some formidable challenges. First of all, we're quite spread out, and we need to coordinate things that are pretty far away."

"You mean you have to 'pass the rocks' to someone on the other side of the stage."

"Right. Then, we're not all engaged in the identical activity. Some of us play very fast notes while others are playing slow notes. Some instruments get their sound out very quickly, but others respond much more slowly—you actually need to start playing them a moment before you want the sound to be heard. And then, we're playing vastly different roles."

"You mean that some are playing melody and others the accompaniment?"

"Yes, that, and even greater differences. Some instruments are terribly busy while others are idle for a period. Yet all of this has to be coordinated with pinpoint precision."

"So how do you do it?"

"It's not easy to achieve, but once you've gotten there it can feel effortless. The musicians need to expand their awareness in both space and time. That means they have to stretch their hearing to include what's going on all around the stage. We talked about that last time, didn't we?

"But, in addition, they need to feel what's coming up as palpably as what is happening now, just like in the rock game. That's why there was so much emphasis today on defining musical goals. It's a way of clarifying where all of this is going—another way of making the future feel more present."

"Is that what you meant when you asked the violins to tell the whole story of the melody?"

"Yes, and when I asked them not to milk every nuance, that

was about making the whole more important than the detail. If a musician's focus on the sound he's making at the moment eclipses his awareness of where the melody is going, then the music will never soar. It will get stodgy—seem to be stuck. You know, even great music can actually sound pretty boring if you lose the thread of the continuity."

"How would that happen?"

"Well, say a clarinetist shares a beautiful tune with two other instruments. Suppose the flute begins, then the clarinet takes over, who finally passes it to the oboe. What if the clarinetist gets so engrossed in reading his own part that he forgets to listen carefully to the others? Then when he makes his entrance he plays it like a beginning. After all, it *is* the beginning of *his* part. But the moment the clarinet takes over, the musical line has been broken. Whatever impetus the flute has created falls flat because the clarinet doesn't continue it. The soaring melody has had it wings clipped and falls to earth. The exact same thing could well happen if the clarinetist plays his final notes like an ending, instead of handing off the energy to the oboist.

"Now, in reality," he continued, "this would probably never happen with professional flute, oboe, and clarinet players because they sit so close to one another. But sections that are quite far removed from each other, they can easily lose awareness of each other's music."

The conductor's words sparked a moment of clarity for me, and I connected the dots. The clarinet handing off the tune to the oboe—wasn't that just like purchasing handing off its work to accounts payable? The collaborative sharing of the melody— why, that's how those two divisions should be thinking about their work: a single tune that gets passed from one part of the stage to another. These handoffs were the very places in the company's process where rocks would pile up, causing errors, which in turn caused more pileups.

Every attempt that we'd made to solve this problem involved finding the place where the rocks were piling up and trying to repair the damage there. But the pileup was merely the location of the problem, not its source. The pileup resulted from departments not having a clear idea of who their partners were, or what the next group did with the information once it was passed to them.

Now my interest in the conductor's ideas went far beyond curiosity. "So how does a conductor handle this?" I asked.

"Well, first of all a conductor must understand what flow is really all about. Many leaders don't realize the power that it has."

I thought about how, only a few minutes ago, I myself had belittled its importance.

"Establishing the flow alone can accomplish more than you can by correcting twenty-five details individually," he concluded.

His words challenged my whole method for solving problems: putting the pieces of the puzzle together, one by one. "How can that be?"

"Well, yes, sometimes it may be useful to break a process down into its minute parts, and fix each one separately. But," he emphasized, "that has never helped anyone to learn to ride a bike."

He could see that he'd really lost me with the bike metaphor and ventured to explain.

"The first few times a child gets on a two-wheel bicycle to learn to ride she can't quite believe that there's any way she'll stay upright. It's only when she gets it moving fast enough that a force is generated powerful enough to hold her up. That's just the way it is with musical flow. When there is enough flow, an invisible but powerful current of energy is produced and felt all over the stage, and even into the hall. That force snaps most everything into place. It enables the musicians to effortlessly avoid most of their errors, and to fix those that do occur much faster and more effectively than by the conductor stopping, breaking things down, and fixing each detail in isolation."

"Okay, I understand the bicycle. But how does that force work with a group of people?"

"Think about the rock game. Once the electricity begins to flow around the circle, people aren't focusing on themselves anymore. They're fitting their individual task into the pulse created by the entire group. That's how flow, by expanding people's awareness to feel the whole, does so much to create a feeling of community."

"So let me just understand how this worked at today's rehearsal." Now I was beginning to get the picture.

"Well, as we've already discussed, people need to clearly know the goals—what they are working toward. This is why I spent so much time today reminding the musicians of the larger goal of each phrase. Otherwise, they would naturally stay preoccupied with the notes on the page in front of them. The leader can do a lot to help them expand their awareness."

His words helped me to realize that the people at purchasing were consumed with accuracy, speed, and compliance with department standards for filling out their forms. They probably had no clue that those very actions would eventually cause a delay in the payment of our suppliers, and ultimately make it harder for the company to stay competitive. They likely saw their role as simply facilitating the procurement of the goods, with no concern for supporting the entire process. If they could truly see beyond their own bailiwick all the way downstream to the company's relationship with its suppliers, they would never tolerate the poor handoff to accounts payable.

My eyes widened when it once again dawned on me that the actual source of the dysfunction was *my leadership vacuum*. I'd never considered that one of my responsibilities was to look after the flow of the process. I'd always been too busy putting out fires on the scene of the latest pileup. Both parties in this breakdown needed the intervention and involvement of a leader before I could expect efficiency to improve. If one of them should try to take charge of the handoff, he would be over-reaching his authority, and every organization has a taboo against that. Only the leader has a wide enough influence to be accountable for flow across the boundaries of the organization.

I shook the maestro's hand and we parted.

So many impressions played over and over in my memory as I drove home. I remembered the way the sound swirled all around the stage, so many people collaborating in it, so seamlessly. And it occurred to me that the vibrations of sound were just a very special form of information that circulated around the orchestra.

I suddenly saw my company as a huge orchestra. When we played, however, it wasn't sound that came out, but information or materials that needed to be shared immediately with our colleagues. Improving the flow in my own "orchestra" would give me the alternative I wanted to my hub-and-spoke approach to the problems we faced. And it might engage the best efforts of our people in solving many of our problems on their own, and perhaps raising our entire performance.

I still had many questions about what I'd heard from the conductor, but it was clear to me that some doable solutions to my problems were beginning to emerge. For the moment I was certain what would be the next item on my to-do list. And as I drove home I was already composing the talk I would give to the heads of accounts payable and purchasing the next day.

We Can't Work It Out

IT WAS COMMON KNOWLEDGE AT THE OFFICE THAT NO one was more dedicated to the company than Mike, the head of manufacturing. He was an expert on the machinery in our plants, and over the years he'd devised many brilliant ways to lower our costs per item we produced and speed up our production schedules. Now, in these lean times, he'd become quite protective of the efficiency he'd worked so hard to achieve. Perhaps too protective.

There were raised voices at our frequent interdepartmental meetings, but the loudest was Rick in sales.

"Mike, we need that new product before the end of the year. Your test schedule is killing us," he'd shouted at last Tuesday's meeting.

Now that sales felt in closer contact with our customers, they were under much pressure to deliver on the new products and services that we had been promising. As our busiest season approached, sales was sounding the alarm that we needed to respond with the new products *now*. Not only had they clarified how we might best respond to our customer's evolving needs as I'd asked, they had taken the initiative to reach out to R&D, and had found a project, already in our pipeline, that was a perfect match.

Now Mike was slowing them down—perhaps fatally. Rick was adamant. He had just gotten wind that the competition was at work developing a similar product and we were in a foot race. Our new product had to be put on the fast track. But when Mike learned that producing the new product would require retooling the plants and losing some of their hard-won efficiency, he dug in his heels.

"I'm not going to compromise quality just to meet your latest deadline," he retorted.

Back in my office later on I reflected on that morning's nastiness. I was so frustrated to see another round of bickering erupt during a meeting—another opportunity for progress derailed. Why was it so difficult for these people to see beyond their parochial concerns! Yes, each branch of the organization was responding to the critical need to improve our balance sheet. But the debate was polluted with mistrust and demonizing of opposing points of view. We were stalemated by zero-sum thinking: if one part of the organization got what it wanted, then the others felt that they were losing.

It was maddeningly obvious to me: when members of a team see the totality of a problem just as clearly as their own part, then they can find breakthrough solutions that accommodate everyone's concerns. Why wasn't that happening? And what could I do about it?

A reminder on my computer chimed, and I suddenly realized that I was due at the conductor's office for a prerehearsal talk in fifteen minutes. So I slammed my laptop closed, grabbed my coat, and ran for the car.

The View from the Chairs

WHEN I SHOWED UP AT THE MAESTRO'S DOOR HE WAS ready for me. "Today I suggest that you sit in a number of different seats throughout the rehearsal," he said.

"In different seats?" I'd grown so used to sitting in one particular chair that I was not very eager to change. "When should I change places?"

"When there's a quiet moment. Try not to disturb anyone. Just find another unoccupied chair and listen from there."

"Why are you suggesting I do that?"

"I think you'll be impressed by how different the sound is from one place to another. We musicians like to say that we see with our ears, and I would like you to experience the orchestra from another section's point of view."

"What do you mean by seeing with your ears?"

"Think of how we normally use our eyes in everyday life: to discover the world around us, to locate ourselves in space, to be aware of what's happening, to make judgments about how to act. In music, all of these functions are performed by the ear. Just take my word for it. You'll understand soon enough."

I was about to ask another question when he suddenly stood up and politely invited me onto the stage. Sure enough, I could hear the oboe playing the A, indicating that the orchestra was tuning up and the rehearsal had begun. I followed the conductor out of his dressing room, and as he made his way to the podium I took a chair and placed it in the back of the orchestra, behind the French horns.

The rehearsal began quickly and I immediately knew the maestro was right; I could certainly see with my ears—or *not* see. I had gotten so used to the sound in the viola section that I felt disoriented and confused in a new chair. Where were the strings? They sounded so distant and dull. It took me a few minutes to construct a new reality from this chair, to know where the various sounds would be coming from.

I also noticed that the kind of music the horns played was quite different from what I'd grown used to hearing. Their first passage consisted of only one note, repeated again and again in the same rhythm. Only two of the four musicians were playing; that struck me as strange, too. Then they all rested in silence for so long that I was just beginning to feel a little restless, when they put their instruments to their lips and all four began to play again. They made a crescendo, and I could hear absolutely *nothing* except horns. Even the trumpets and drums were barely audible when the horns were playing.

The next time the conductor stopped the musicians I slipped away from the horns and around the perimeter of the orchestra until I reached the double-bass section. I realized that these musicians were all perched on stools because their instruments are so big that they can't possibly sit down while playing. So I decided to stand. Already this was a different world, and they hadn't played a note yet.

When the orchestra started again the bass players put down their bows and began to pluck their strings. I was surprised by how strange and different the sound of the orchestra was from here. From where I stood I could see that one of the horn players had the melody, but frankly I could barely hear him because all the cellos in front were playing the same tune, and drowning him out.

From the demeanor of the bass players I could tell that this was not a very challenging passage—they didn't seem to have much to do. But then came one awkward note, and for a split second it sounded pretty sour to me. Instantly I felt the conductor's eyes leap across the room toward us. With all the sound in this room, I wondered, could he have heard that?

During the intermission the conductor pulled me aside for a moment and suggested that I sit near the first violins. Then he set up a chair about ten feet behind his podium, at the edge of the stage, and said that I should end the rehearsal there.

After the break they began with the second movement of the piece. I couldn't keep my eyes off the quick but subtle movements of the bow of the violinist sitting next to me. It seemed to be bouncing ever so slightly and repeatedly in the same place, and the sound it produced was delicate, yet precise. I thought that this must be quite difficult to learn to do, but when I glanced at his right hand it seemed very relaxed. Then I noticed that the other nine players were doing exactly the same thing. What amazing timing, I thought. This was no piece of cake to coordinate.

Eventually the string section paused, but the violins were not nearly as chatty with one another as the horns or the basses had been. At first I assumed they were simply unsociable, but I began to understand that this movement required them to maintain their focus even when they weren't playing. One player's late entrance could throw the section into turmoil, and everyone seemed to understand that.

Finally I moved to the chair behind the podium. The conductor had been so right in asking me to end up here. From this position I could see each of the chairs in which I had sat, and then think about the sound as I heard it there. What I heard now was much more than the sum of those various realities.

Everything, every section, even every player was audible now, but in exactly the proportion that made the whole of the music come alive.

I suppose I had always known, in a logical way, that an orchestra is a dynamic, everchanging image in sound, in which all the parts are constantly rearranging to allow the listener to hear what matters most in the music. But from this new point of view the foreground, middle ground, and background sounds snapped into focus as if a two-dimensional photo was suddenly turned into a three-dimensional hologram before my eyes. I sat spellbound before the music's changing texture. I was seeing with my ears.

After the rehearsal the conductor asked me, "So did your sitting in different chairs show you anything that surprised you?"

"Did it ever!" I exclaimed. "It wasn't just a trivial difference. It was startling how different the reality of the music is from different chairs."

"What could you tell about the different roles played by different sections?"

"Well, I would say that the brass and kettledrums play a more supporting role. They sometimes remain silent for a while. But when they do come in, their sound is quite dominant."

"Yes, go on," he said. "What about the basses?"

"Their part doesn't seem so important when you stand in their section, but when you hear the whole orchestra you realize how indispensable they are."

"Yes, you see how much they are all role players in the piece as a whole. But their roles are different, their sound is different, their responsibilities are different. And each player cannot help but identify with the experience of the orchestra from that particular chair, right?"

"Sure, of course."

"And yet when you moved behind the podium?" he said, urging me to go on.

"What an incredible difference. I could hear it all. No, no," I said with animation, "it wasn't just that I could hear it all. I heard it all in the right proportion. It all fit together, it all made sense. It all mixed together so beautifully."

"So can you see what all of this means?" he said, looking excited himself, and very expectant.

It was all overwhelming. I felt that my body had been resonated, like a bell that's been rung. Although the sound was now gone, the sensation remained like an electric charge. But I couldn't find any more words.

"Come with me." I followed him out of the dressing room, back into the hall, where the empty stage was still set up. The chairs and stands were in that particular array, somewhat like an amphitheater, which I had come to recognize as the orchestra's setup. He then invited me to stand on the podium.

The View from the Podium

I'D NEVER BEEN ON A CONDUCTOR'S PODIUM, AND WAS surprised how much difference a one-foot platform made. The stage lay before me like a panorama from a hilltop. I had a direct sight line to each and every chair. I tried to locate each chair in which I had sat during the rehearsal, one by one. Then I saw that he was watching me.

"That's right," he said, understanding immediately what I was doing. "Do you recall the way the music sounded from each chair?"

I nodded. The sound of the orchestra was still in my memory.

"Can you imagine how it would sound from up here? Can you imagine the sound with all the instruments not only playing, but also projecting their sound toward you? Look at the way the room is laid out. See how the podium is the focal point, both visually and acoustically?"

I nodded again. From up here I noticed how each string section was laid out in straight lines that intersected at the podium.

"Can you imagine the clarity, the brilliance, the sheer volume of the sound up here? When you were seated with the players your ear was at the level of where the sound is produced.

Naturally you heard most clearly the instrument that was nearest you. And even when you sat behind the podium you were still slightly below where you are now. But standing up here, your ear is perhaps four feet higher. You hear the individual sounds, but you also hear what happens above the players' heads, where their sounds mix and blend together."

"It must be overwhelming," I said. "There must be so much to listen to."

"There's a lot of sound to navigate through, which is why we conductors have to develop such penetrating hearing. But musicians must listen and play at the same time, and make many musical judgments based on what they hear. You sat in those chairs less than an hour ago. And you moved from chair to chair. You heard how utterly different the sound was from each position. You heard exactly what the musicians in the nearby chairs heard. So you understand that each musician has an entirely different reality, a different set of facts on which to make his decisions about how to play.

"Now here's the key point. When a player has sat in the same chair for a long time, he will unconsciously assume that everyone can, and probably does, hear what he hears. He'll take for granted that everyone experiences the same reality. And," he added with emphasis, "he is quite unaware of what he himself does *not* hear and of who can't hear *him*!"

I nodded in recognition. Standing there on the podium, scanning the big picture of the orchestra, a new and startling realization was dawning on me. The members of my leadership team were such experts in their respective fields. It had never occurred to me that they might be completely unaware of the reality that was staring me in the face. With respect to them I stood on a kind of podium that enabled me to see a different picture of our organization.

They might have been obliquely aware of the problems of

the company as a whole, but to them these problems seemed abstract and distant, eclipsed by the pressing issues that preoccupied them every day. No wonder they hadn't yet seen the need for the kind of collaboration I was envisioning. It was easy enough for me to imagine the various pieces of our company puzzle falling together into a coherent strategy, because I was on the podium. I was in the ideal position to make sense of it all. I was aware of the combined activities of all the departments. And I carelessly assumed that they were seeing what I was seeing.

The quarrels and disputes that broke out during meetings suddenly made perfect sense to me. No wonder Mike had gotten so defensive about his manufacturing schedule. After all, when I'd sat near the horn section I had no way of hearing the whole orchestra either.

"Do the musicians have any idea what the conductor hears?" I asked.

"Hardly any of them have ever stood on a podium while an orchestra was playing. So, no, they don't. And this profound difference in point of view between podium and chair invites continual misunderstanding. Things that are obvious from the podium may be totally imperceptible from the chair. If a conductor is not experienced he may grow frustrated with a player for something that the musician has no awareness of doing or neglecting to do. Let that frustration come into your voice even a little and you erode the shared ownership of the music that you've worked so hard to achieve."

I blushed a bit at the thought of my own frustration with my people. "Does that ever happen?"

"Does it ever! It's commonplace. Let me tell you a true story. I lived it myself." He went over to the double-bass section and brought back a stool for me to sit on.

"I remember," he said, "when I was a student at the conservatory. They had an orchestra for the conducting students to learn on. At the time I'd decided I needed to know more about the string instruments and was taking lessons in viola. So one day while one of my fellow students was conducting I took a seat in the viola section and actually joined them in playing. I was thunderstruck by the skill of the young musicians around me. Their hands were supple; their sound was pure and round; their facility with the instrument seemed flawless. From my novice level of playing I truly felt like I was sitting among geniuses.

"After the intermission, it was my turn to conduct. We were playing a complicated twentieth-century work, and the orchestra wasn't familiar with it. I, carrying the responsibility that comes with the podium, of course, had studied it quite thoroughly. As we played through it, these same violists, at whose feet I had been ready to worship twenty minutes ago, now seemed like simpletons, bumbling fools who had no clue about music. Even I was a bit shocked by the disdain that I felt welling up in me. I had to laugh at myself."

Remembering how naïve and inexperienced he had once been, the maestro enjoyed a self-effacing laugh. He had no idea how his cheerful words had inspired such deep introspection on my part.

"If, as you say," I ventured seriously, "the difference between podium and chair invites continual misunderstanding, how can that be avoided?"

"It's tempting to pass that off onto the players, just as I did that day. But I believe that it is the conductor's responsibility," he warned. "The conductor is on the podium because he has been given the authority to lead. His job is to create success. It really falls upon him to stretch his reality until it encompasses that of the players, too."

"But wait," I interjected. "I can see why the players need to stretch their awareness to encompass the podium point of view. But you seem to be saying the opposite, that the conductor needs to understand the reality from the chairs as well."

"Yes, I am," he said with certitude. "It's easy to feel that the podium reality is the best reality—the most far-reaching and comprehensive. But that's a trap, and if you fall into it you may lose the confidence and respect of your team."

"I don't understand," I objected. "How can grasping the big picture be a trap?"

"It can be," he said, "if you discount the importance of the reality from the chair. Yes, the podium offers you a unique vantage point on your orchestra, your group. But the reality from the chair is what the players have to deal with day in and day out. It's ironic, maybe, but if a conductor wants them to play with unity then he must stretch his imagination to embrace their reality. That's what elicits the kind of cooperation and trust that invites them to get interested in the unique perspective the podium offers."

So instead of getting frustrated with Mike's stubborn resistance to seeing my point of view, I needed to get more genuinely curious about his. And Rick's, too. Was there something crucial that I wasn't seeing from my office? And maybe my interest in each of them might soften their intransigence toward each other.

The maestro continued.

"This is the way that the podium can be used for the orchestra's benefit. When an orchestra plays there is a great deal of communicating and collaborating going on. The musicians will do this by themselves, but they can be greatly aided by a conductor who is sensitive to their needs. Often they may not know the best person with whom to make ensemble or they may know but not be able to hear them."

"Why would they not know the best person to listen to?"

"You remember what you heard inside the orchestra. Each chair is influenced by its location. So every musician tends to navigate his or her course based on those sounds that are readily available. Generally, that means the people close to you. But the more fruitful musical partnerships that I discover on the page of the score or from the height of the podium may not be at all evident from the chairs. However, once such things are pointed out, in the right way, the musicians are perfectly capable of reaching their ears across the stage, as you have seen many times in our rehearsals."

"Another thing I noticed when I sat behind the horns was that the orchestra became a large collection of the backs of people's heads. Up here I would see all the faces."

"That's right," he exclaimed, "including the *expressions* on their faces. And so, from the podium, you have access to all the resources available."

This gave me a clue as to why I trusted all the people on my own leadership team, but they didn't necessarily trust one another. My position allowed me to see what each part contributed to the whole. The members of the team, however, were surprisingly unaware of the support they received from others, but hyperaware of any threat posed by the invisible activity in another building or wing.

As I looked out around the stage once again I was pondering whether I was doing all that I could to share what I knew from my "podium." As my eyes fell on each chair I tried to imagine the way the music might sound there. Then I had a sudden insight: certain problems can be solved most easily from the chair, but others require the podium view.

If a machine breaks down at one of Mike's factories, for example, we don't need the buyers, planners, or customer service people to collaborate on the solution. When it's an innately local, technical issue, all we need is a local, technical expert.

However, when it is an issue about collaboration across the company, as with Mike and Rick, then it becomes a system problem, which can most easily be comprehended from the podium. As their leader I cannot just throw up my hands in frustration at their inability to grapple with systemic problems. They needed me to engage and bridge the gap between the podium and the chair.

"Well," the conductor said, gesturing for me to give him back the double-bass stool, "I think you've begun to make friends with the podium today. It takes quite a bit of getting used to."

He returned the stool and led me out the door. I was already in my own world thinking about the next day's schedule and how I could fit in a face-to-face with Mike and Rick. I knew I had to talk to them while this experience was still fresh and my mind was brimming with ideas about how to help them.

Suddenly the maestro stopped and turned to me. "I almost forgot! A colleague of mine who teaches at the conservatory has been called out of town and has asked me to take one of his conducting classes. I think it might be very interesting for you."

The Pep Talk

THE NEXT REGULAR MEETING WITH ALL OF MY DEPART-
ment heads was upon me before I knew it, and I was well
aware that this was going to be an important one. Despite
making some impressive strides toward our goals, we had suffered two more months of weak sales. I sensed that the team
needed the assurance of a steady hand at the helm. And I
wanted to bolster their confidence by showing that I was on
top of the situation. I'd come to understand that, being on the
podium, I could see the strategic issues more clearly than the
members of the team. So I planned a crisp agenda, and was
determined not to be sidetracked by anything that could turn
into another squabble.

When the team arrived and gathered around our conference
table, I began by congratulating everyone on the progress the
team had been making. I noted how much better they were
listening to and communicating with each other and with our
customers and suppliers.

But then came the tough love. I described our major disap-
pointments, one by one, explaining what mistakes had been
made and how they had contributed to our difficulties. For the
most part the group listened, but occasionally someone would
bring up a peripheral matter.

"Listen," I said, keeping a tight rein on the meeting, "we've got a lot of important topics to cover, and I want to stay with the agenda. We're limiting the discussion to only strategic matters today."

I was so well prepared, in fact, that when an occasional question was raised I was ready with the answer. "I'm feeling a little uncomfortable with the numbers we're seeing from our distributors," John ventured.

"You're right, John," I replied. I'd already reached the conclusion that we might well need to make a change. "So you think that we should find one or two new distribution partners? I probably agree with you." Then I proposed a plan, appointing a role for each team member.

When I'd finished covering the agenda, I looked around the room and waited for some reaction. The room was quiet. Not one of them was showing any spark or passion about getting back on top. Clearly I needed to fire them up a bit.

"Come on, guys, we've been behind for two quarters now." I raised my voice. "We've got good products and we're introducing new products, so why aren't we doing better?" I didn't wait for a response. "This can't continue. I want you to get behind this and push harder. Put more pressure on the distributors. If they can't do it, we'll have to find someone else."

The hour was up. I thanked them all for coming, and they filed out of the room, making idle conversation. I can't say that it was a great meeting. It probably wasn't very pleasant for them to hear all of this bad news, but I got the job done. We covered everything. That's what I get paid for.

ALL WEEK I HAD BEEN LOOKING FORWARD TO MY NEXT visit with the maestro, this time at the conservatory. I made my way down a quiet tree-lined street to my destination, a large rehearsal studio inside a grand brick building on the grounds of the university. Inside, college-age musicians were arriving and unpacking their instruments.

My visits to the orchestra rehearsals these months had made me quite preoccupied with the art of conducting, so I was very curious about what a conducting lesson would be like. I'd learned a great deal about how the conductor prepares for rehearsals, communicates his vision to his players, engages their talent, monitors their playing through acute listening, creates a sense of community, and helps everyone grasp the big picture.

There was, however, one aspect of conducting that still puzzled me. What role does the baton play in this complex relationship between the conductor and the musicians? The maestro had already proved to me that it wasn't like the mainspring of a clock, generating power to drive the gears. But I'd never had the occasion to ask him about its true power.

I would sometimes scrutinize the maestro's gestures, trying to understand which motions corresponded to certain outcomes in the music. Though I still could not decode its secret language, it was clear to me that the maestro's baton cast a kind of spell over the orchestra. Sometimes I thought of it as a sorcerer's magic wand, with the power to summon the spirits of the great composers. The movements of the baton definitely had a decisive impact on the orchestra, but I didn't understand exactly how it worked. I was optimistic that today's conducting lesson would help me penetrate this mystery.

Gradually the orchestra filled its ranks and the maestro entered, followed by the four conducting students. After the orchestra tuned up, the first student stepped onto the podium. Tall and slender, his blond hair cut in a classic style, the young man had a certain panache that immediately made me want to watch him. He emanated authority and confidence, and seemed to take charge even before he raised his baton.

I have to confess that I became pretty captivated by him. His motions were beautifully coordinated, like a dancer communicating with the orchestra through the movements of his baton. He was the only other conductor I'd watched carefully since I began sitting in at orchestra rehearsals. And, though his conducting looked nothing like the maestro's, I found it stirring.

As the piece came to its rousing ending I was almost expecting applause from somewhere, but the orchestra looked a little ho-hum. This surprised me, and I was curious to hear what the maestro had to say.

He came forward from behind the first violins. "Well, this is a very talented young man," he declared.

When he reached the podium he laid his hand on the student's shoulder in a reassuring, avuncular gesture. "You have an uncommon gift for movement, and the ability to project great energy. You also display considerable musical intelligence. All of this is very good."

Then he turned to face the student straight on. "But there is something missing, and it is such an important deficiency that it could block all the rest of your talent from ever truly touching the orchestra."

The student looked a bit stunned to hear such a fundamental criticism.

"You see," he continued, "most people might not be able to tell, but I can clearly see that you are not really listening to the orchestra."

The student raised his eyebrows, looking ready to object, but the maestro had read his mind. "Yes, I know that you were engaged with the music. That was quite evident from the power of your concentration and the beauty of your movements. But I don't believe that you were truly hearing *these* musicians as they played right here and now."

The student blinked.

"I understand," the conductor resumed. "Hearing an orchestra is not an easy thing to do. There are so many different parts to listen to, and just taking in how they fit together is quite a task. But a conductor must hear exactly how those parts were just played. Of course, that involves noticing any mistakes and flaws. But you must also hear and appreciate all that was good in the playing. Unless you cultivate this kind of listening, orchestras will never play to you. They won't be drawn out by the magnetic power of your attentive ear. If musicians don't see that you are affected by their musical ideas, they will be neither inspired nor able to sustain their highest level of energy and confidence."

"But," the student said, "I thought that it's all about how the orchestra reacts to the conductor, not the other way around."

"Ah, but this is a young man's mistake." Now the maestro went over to his briefcase, pulled out a book, and thumbed through the pages.

"Yes, here it is: from the memoirs of Georg Solti, longtime conductor of the Chicago Symphony. He talks about how early in his career he had terrible problems with great orchestras, such as the Vienna Philharmonic. 'I freely admit,' he writes, 'that part of my difficulties in Vienna were of my own making. Although I was forty-five years old, I had only eleven years of solid conducting experience behind me. I had not yet learned that as a conductor, one's first task is not to stamp one's own personality on everything, at whatever cost, but to listen. Today, if an orchestra gives me something that is better than what I had in mind, I recognize it and gratefully adopt it, but forty years ago, I did not understand such things.' "

The student nodded, trying to absorb all of this. "What did Solti mean," he asked, "when he said that a conductor's first task is to listen? That sounds so simple. What do you listen for?"

"Well, I listen for many things. How well the orchestra knows this piece. If they have performed it before. Whether they know it so well that they are listening and working together across the orchestra. If this is their first time reading the music, how quickly they are learning it as they play. If there are any great artists in the group whose playing could inspire all the rest. As I conduct I explore these and many other clues. Depending on what I find, I adjust the way I use the baton so that it uniquely suits the circumstances before me."

He once again touched the student's shoulder reassuringly. "Today I watched you conduct and listened to the orchestra react. Even though I sensed a powerful artist in you, I saw that the orchestra wasn't really responding. Your beautiful, polished gestures were not changing and adapting around the orchestra's playing, responding to what they were offering."

I winced a bit for the student. But then my second reaction was that this lesson, though painful, would probably save him from many mistakes, and enable him to become a much more effective leader.

"You see," said the maestro, "it is a wonderful thing to project confidence and authority. But your main channel of influence with an orchestra is your listening."

"I thought it was the beat in your baton," the student suggested.

"Of course, you're right, the beat in your baton is important." The maestro rubbed his chin, pondering how to explain. Then he looked up and asked, "Do you know what a click track is?"

"Yes, I once played on a recording of the sound track for a film, and we used a click track. Everyone wore headphones and listened to the same metronomic pulse. Only by controlling the pulse mechanically can the music be precisely synchronized to a film image."

"Exactly. So you know from experience that an orchestra can play perfectly well with a click track. Was it great music-making, in your opinion?"

"Well, it was a great group of top recording musicians, and a very good paycheck, so that was exciting. But, no, it didn't feel like any art was being made. It felt more like being a cog in some assembly line, mass-producing interchangeable parts. There was no life to it, no emotion."

"Why do you think that was?" the conductor probed.

The student was at a loss for words. "I don't know. A click track is a machine. You know, no matter how you play it's never going to vary. Since it doesn't respond to you, you automatically become a bit more like a machine yourself. I mean the playing is accurate, but it can't have soul."

"So, in order to play with 'soul,' as you put it, you need the pulse to be responsive, right?" the conductor asked pointedly. "When the musicians feel that the pulse is unresponsive, they play in a more mechanical manner. Since artists don't particularly like being treated as cogs in a machine, they unconsciously choose to turn themselves off. Their minds wander, their sounds lose the luster and depth of their tone."

"You know, you're right. That's exactly what happened to me at that recording session."

"And that's what happens to an orchestra when a conductor's baton does not react to their sound in real time."

"Maestro, was my conducting really no better than a click track?"

"No." He smiled warmly at the student. "Of course you were much, much better. That's why you have so much promise. But in spite of all the expertise you invest in your leadership, if you don't listen as well as you move that baton, orchestras will not be able to summon their most artistic playing, even if they want to.

"Every time you come to the podium, ask yourself, 'Am I really hearing what's going on in this room? Am I being affected by what I'm hearing?' If not, then you must take some of your attention away from what you yourself are doing, and focus it on the people you're here to lead."

These words touched me deeply, as if I were the student myself and my flaws were being dissected. Until that moment I hadn't thought twice about my behavior at the meeting this morning. Now I saw that my preoccupation with putting on a display of strong leadership had completely distracted me from listening to the team.

I grimaced at the painful memory of John's remark about the distribution numbers. I had not really heard him at all. Instead I used his comment as a launching pad to state the conclusions I had already drawn. I had made the beginning conductor's mistake of believing that impressing my authority and personality on the group was good leadership. The more I replayed the meeting, the more I realized that I had studiously cut myself off from every opportunity to hear what my team was thinking.

Don't Oversee Every Note

THE SOUND OF THE ORCHESTRA RETUNING BROUGHT MY attention back into the room, and the second student conductor appeared on the podium. He was a dark-haired young man with an intelligent presence and energetic bearing. His conducting projected a nervy and vigorous alertness, and his attention seemed to be everywhere, eyes darting from one section of the orchestra to another. In fact, I noticed that he was making very keen and focused eye contact with the musicians. I had no doubt that *he* was listening. He seemed to be aware of every note that the orchestra was playing.

I realized after a few moments that it was more than just awareness that this student was projecting—he was in fact directing every detail in the score. His movements articulated every entrance, every note, every crescendo. That was pretty impressive to me, to be able to show so much information in such a short time. The orchestra's energy seemed high, and the playing was very neat and tidy. Nothing sounded out of place. I was impressed with his control. After the piece finished he turned expectantly to the maestro.

"Excellent energy," the maestro commented. "Very good knowledge of the details of the score—extremely accurate rhythm and a very articulate baton. Bravo." The student tried, without success, to contain his pleasure at these words.

"And yet," he said, finished with his compliments, "the orchestra will hate playing for you if you continue to conduct this way."

The student stared blankly at the maestro, who continued in a kind tone of voice.

"You are clearly very dedicated and well prepared. Not only do you know each and every note in the score, but your conducting actively *demonstrates* that you do. Every time a new instrument plays you give a cue. That's very worthy of you. But what real value is all of that adding? Let's see what the orchestra can do entirely without you."

He turned to the orchestra and said, "Ladies and gentlemen, would you please play from the beginning—this time *without* the conductor."

The group of young musicians looked a bit confused and sheepish, but many were also shooting amused looks around the orchestra as they prepared to do something that evidently had never been asked of them. I noticed many of them looking at the concertmaster, a young violinist. He waited for the group's concentration, and then lifted his bow. At once the entire orchestra was playing with assurance and authority, and quite together, just as the professionals had done at my very first rehearsal with the maestro.

The conducting student stood to the side and watched as the musicians played through the first five minutes of the piece. Then the maestro stopped them. There was high energy in the orchestra. It seemed that some had enjoyed it very much, while others seemed to heave a sigh of relief that the exercise was over. But whatever their reaction, it had changed the dynamic among them. They were a unified group in a way they hadn't been before.

"Now," said the maestro, smiling himself, "let's consider what this means. All this caretaking you were doing for the orchestra: at the very least, it's debatable whether they actually needed it. So let me ask you," he said, making his way through the orchestra until he reached one of the horn players, "you're pretty far from the podium. I was listening carefully and you were playing exactly in time with the violins. How did you do that?"

The horn player wore a bemused smile, and hesitated before speaking. "Well," she finally said, "we watched the concertmaster for the opening cue. Then we listened really carefully, and followed whatever we needed to." At these words the players shuffled their feet, a spontaneous sign of approval among musicians, who can't use their hands to applaud. Clearly this exercise had aroused a heightened level of interest throughout the orchestra.

"So," said the maestro to the conductor, "you heard the orchestra play just now: no cues from you, no caring for each detail the way you did. And yet they played this piece very well. So let's ask ourselves what they need the baton for."

There was a pregnant silence. Finally the maestro broke it. "Would you mind if I borrowed your baton?" he asked the student. Then he stepped up to the podium and signaled the orchestra to get ready to play.

Out came the same music, but with a fresh momentum and dramatic energy that had been entirely lacking in the previous playing. This time the music seemed to have its own power, like a marionette that has broken free of its master's strings and miraculously started to move by its own life force. The difference was striking and clearly impressed both the student conductor and the young musicians in the orchestra.

"Now may I conduct the same passage again, imitating what I saw you do?" This time the maestro's gestures were not what I had come to expect from him. While not overtly awkward, they were also not what I would call natural; his eyes were darting skittishly around the orchestra, much as the student's had. The music sounded stiff and contrived—a puppet on a string. When he stopped he turned to the student and asked, "So what was the difference? Could you hear it?"

"I heard it for sure," he said in a bewildered voice, "but I can't say how you did it."

"Well, let's try to understand this. When you conducted you were certainly engaged and concentrated. The trouble was that you were engaged in leading the orchestra through actions for which they did not need you! It's important to make a distinction between problems that the musicians can best solve themselves, and problems that involve collaboration and teamwork. When your baton undertakes to solve every problem that might arise, you actually decrease the orchestra's listening ability. But when there was nobody on the podium, that forced them to work together, and they played better than when you conducted."

The student tried his best to conceal his puzzlement.

"Now," said the maestro in a reassuring voice, "I know that as a conductor you feel responsible to oversee every note. But to the musicians such behavior reads that you do not trust them to do their own jobs."

Immediately there was another shuffle from the musicians.

"You see, that's why they would quickly grow to hate working with you. They would feel smothered, repressed, and undervalued."

"Then what did you do just now to get such an amazing result?"

"Aha! I, too, was engaged and concentrated, but I concentrated on a different mission. Even before I lifted the baton I was absorbed in my most beautiful vision of how this music could sound. I filled my imagination with that image, and through my baton offered it to the orchestra, and trusted them to take care of the details and do what was necessary to make the vision a reality." He looked out at the players. "And, as you heard, they did."

"But how do you know that they will? How can you be sure?"

Then the maestro brought up the bicycle analogy, just as he had explained it to me during our conversation about flow. "Your instinct tells you that by moving forward you will fall off the bike. But it is only in letting go, and trusting that somehow some force will appear that will keep you upright, that you can ever learn to ride. Trusting the orchestra feels that way at the beginning. You must create the flow of the music, and leave to the musicians the playing of the notes.

"That is why your eye contact was so disruptive to them. It splintered the flow. It sent the message that flow is less important than the notes. But the flow and the details must both be there for the music to come to life."

The student stood there, trying to absorb such a rich and profound lesson. "Come!" said the conductor, breaking the spell of his own words. "You try it now."

We could all see that it was awkward for the student, so the maestro explained how to focus on his vision, hear it inwardly before raising his baton, and keep hearing what was next, even while the orchestra was playing. After a few tries something fundamental had seemed to shift for this student. And when he finally stopped the orchestra, I felt the approval in the room.

With this revelation it was time for a break, and the maestro called for intermission.

Once again my conscience was heavy with thoughts of this morning's meeting. Looking back with the wisdom of hindsight I realized that the team was probably already pretty well aware of all the items on the agenda. There might have been some small value added by having them hear my point of view.

But I missed the far greater opportunity to be had in letting them grapple with those problems collectively. By insisting that the discussion unfold strictly within the boundaries I'd set, I suppressed the team. And whatever headway I'd made by highlighting their recent progress I lost when I squashed the contributions they were trying to make at that very meeting.

As the details of the meeting came back to me I slapped myself on the forehead. All the dialogue had been one-on-one: between me and one member of the team. There had been no cross-fertilization of ideas—no sharing of information or perspectives among them. Just like this student conductor, my behavior grew out of dedication to doing a good job. Yet instead I had conveyed an attitude of mistrust and lack of confidence in my group.

I felt a gentle tap on my shoulder. The maestro was inviting me to join him and the four students in the cafeteria for some coffee. When we all sat down they had many questions for him.

"When the orchestra played without a conductor, they were able to manage on this piece. But what about when they can't manage without you?"

"Excellent question," he replied after finishing a sip from his cup. "An amateur orchestra, for example, needs much more hands-on direction from its conductor. But you four are learning how to conduct first-class professional orchestras. I want to acquaint you with how to lead when the orchestra already knows the music and doesn't need to be taught. That is the most difficult type of leadership to learn. They still need direction if they're ever to perform to their potential, but the direction must be more visionary and strategic and less about helping them manage the details."

"What about when a fine orchestra doesn't know the piece at all?" asked the second student. "What if they've never heard of the composer, and the music is complex and really requires a conductor? Suppose they're under great pressure, like having to make a recording on very little rehearsal time."

"Under those circumstances," he replied, "the kind of hands-on, detailed conducting you did today might success-fully shepherd the musicians through a difficult challenge. So you've always got to take the temperature of your group, moni-tor how they're managing, and decide what kind of leadership they need from you. You must have many different styles and approaches available, and always be looking to expand your range."

It didn't take much imagination for me to translate this whole discussion into the vocabulary of my business. The maestro was talking about micromanagement, a trap that I'd fallen into this very morning. But until this lesson, I hadn't realized that a mi-cromanager's core problem is not too much leadership, but rather too little. His vision and strategy are *withheld* or *never explained*. So the subordinates are either deprived of working toward a larger goal, or constantly in suspense about when, if ever, they will find out what that goal actually is. I didn't say a word to my team about our overarching goal, or how the agenda items I'd chosen connected with it. I just told them what to do.

"Maestro," asked the first student, "it seemed like the orches-tra got better the moment you stepped onto the podium, before a note was played. What did you do, and what did they see?"

"You know," he began in reply, "a mature conductor has been studying and contemplating his repertoire for quite some time. Over the years I've developed a kind of aural picture of how a given work should sound. When I step onto the podium and look around the room I start to imagine what these players would sound like if they adopted my vision. I even start to live that fantasy. It affects my breathing and my facial expressions."

The conducting students weren't sure that he was finished,

and waited for a moment to see if that was all he would say. Then the second student asked, "Is that all? That's all that you did?"

"Well," he said, sounding surprised, "that's really quite a lot. Those first seven seconds on the podium, that's not an empty moment. It is a pregnant moment. If the orchestra can witness the conductor living his dream of the music, then they will feel confident playing it. It all happens so quickly and so silently the orchestra isn't even really aware of it. After all, they're focusing on preparing themselves to play. Yet the transmission of this most essential element of leadership makes all the difference between mediocrity and brilliance."

Had the maestro made this pronouncement an hour and a half earlier I might not have believed it. Now, however, I saw that *this* was the conjuring, the sorcery of a conductor. It was his capacity to dream, and then to embody it and translate that dream into the motions of the baton. The reason it had eluded me was because it happens so fast, and before a note has sounded. It also deceived me because I was looking for something at the moment the orchestra played. By then the process was long over.

The Minimum Is Always Best

WE MADE OUR WAY BACK TO THE REHEARSAL STUDIO, and the third student readied herself to conduct as the orchestra tuned. Like the other two, she wore an expression of alertness, intelligence, and intensity. She raised both arms with energy and launched into her piece. It opened with a vigorous and lively passage, and she threw herself into it with enthusiasm and abandon. Though she was not a tall young woman, her movements seemed larger to me than those of her colleagues, but no less coordinated or agile.

After the last two lessons I thought I knew what to look for in the conductor's performance, and I scrutinized her movements. I felt that she was doing more than just micromanaging. The orchestra played with power and vitality, but somehow I didn't find it very pleasing. I had grown accustomed to the deep and resonant sounds drawn by the maestro from his own orchestra. This playing felt effortful and forced. Then I noticed that she had broken a visible sweat on the podium, which had not happened with the others.

When the piece was over the maestro approached her. "Bravo. You have an excellent feel for this piece, and your love for it comes through."

She gave a slight nod of her head, acknowledging that she felt understood.

"Now the challenge is to get the orchestra to play it as beautifully as you imagine it. I believe that if you heard a recording of this run-through you would be disappointed with the effect. Do you know in what respect you missed your mark?"

She looked perplexed and couldn't answer.

"So," he went on, "let's talk a bit, then, about the podium and the baton. Both of them are amplifiers. The podium is one because it makes the conductor 'larger than life.' This is a good thing, because it provides the platform from which she can influence the entire orchestra without distorting or straining her body. The baton is an amplifier because it takes a small distance traveled by the hand and makes it larger at the tip of the baton. This is also good, because we can make quite small gestures that are still perfectly visible to the orchestra.

"So when you stand on the podium and look out over this vast sea of musicians, your first instinct is to feel that it's necessary to shout to reach all of them. You push and thrust your leadership out so that everyone can read it. But that's unnecessary. The podium and the baton already provide you with ample authority, and you must modulate your message so that it comes across as you intend.

"Let me show you, please," he said, asking her to allow him to join her on the podium. Then he signaled the orchestra to prepare to play, and took his place directly behind her. He took hold of her right hand, in which she held the baton.

"Now allow me, please, to conduct the orchestra with your hand. Just keep your arm totally relaxed, and feel what I do with the baton."

He then proceeded to do a strange pas-de-deux with her, in which he controlled the conducting but she could feel what it was like to make such gestures. After a minute or two he stopped and asked her what she had felt.

"Why, it's so subtle! You really don't have to do much!"

"Yes, it's surprising, isn't it?"

"Very!" she said, still a little overwhelmed with what she'd just experienced. "The baton can affect so much, even with the smallest movements."

"Yes, exactly!" he affirmed. "You don't have to clutch the baton like a mallet. It's a delicate implement, especially when you're working with fine musicians who know their jobs. The power is in them. We don't create that power, we only direct it."

"It's such a different feeling!" she said, still taking it all in.

"Indeed. Herbert von Karajan, longtime conductor of the Berlin Philharmonic, liked to tell a story from his youth. He was learning to ride."

"Horses?" she interjected.

"Yes. And one day his instructor announced that at the next lesson Karajan was going to learn to jump the horse. Karajan confesses to having spent a week of anxiety about how he was ever going to get such a big animal over that hurdle. Then, when the lesson finally came, he learned that it was much easier than he had feared. All you had to do was get the horse to the right place in the right way, and the horse would do the jumping itself. Karajan said that conducting is like that. The orchestra does the executing."

"And when I conducted before, I thought I needed to do the jumping myself," she said, without pretense, revealing what a discovery this was for her.

"Yes. As leaders we should strive to exert the *minimum necessary intervention*. If the orchestra plays with strength and power, it doesn't mean that the conductor has to continually exert. Let the musicians do their job, without feeling that you have to continue to pump them up. As we conduct we constantly explore how much we need to do. Once we've reached that equilibrium, it's time to let go."

"Maestro," she said, "you said the *minimum* necessary intervention?"

"Yes. That will vary. Some orchestras need quite a bit of energy to wake them up, but once awakened, then you can let up. Others are quite sensitive, and can be relied on to take care of themselves. Then you can merely refine what your vision tells you is necessary. The minimum is always best. That way, you encourage your players to cultivate sensitivity, and to communicate with one another. Do you see?" he asked as he invited her down from the podium.

Now I was reflecting on my team's behavior during the meeting. I had failed to understand that their silence was a response to being micromanaged. Instead of hearing the deeper meaning behind that silence I had decided to turn up the intensity with my "pep talk." I hadn't realized the extent to which my seat at the head of the table already amplified the impact of everything I said and did. No wonder they were silent! Their instinctive reaction had been to protect themselves, rather than open up to me and to one another. I saw that I myself had played the leading role in breeding such a stale and stifling atmosphere.

Lead, Don't Cheerlead

THE ORCHESTRA TUNED UP ONCE AGAIN, AND THE FINAL
student stepped up to the podium. He was a good-looking
young man who presented a friendly demeanor. And like the
first conductor, he was very graceful and well coordinated. His
gestures were elegant, energetic, and pleasing to watch. I believed that he was listening, because he certainly did react to
what happened in the orchestra. He impressed me. However,
compared to the energy I had felt during previous rehearsals,
the orchestra seemed limp and bored, but I attributed that to
the inexperience of the conservatory orchestra.

Finally the music came to an end, and the student's eyes
turned toward the maestro, who had stepped forward.

"Very gifted artist," he said warmly. "You have studied the
music well and offered very good attention to the players. All
of this is very good."

He paused, and a sudden stillness filled the room.

"And yet," he continued, gently shaking his head in puzzlement, "the orchestra does not play for you. Your polished conducting does not engage the orchestra at all, and we must figure
out why this is so."

He could see that the student was bewildered, trying to
make sense of this critique.

"Let me show you," he said as he approached the podium, reaching out his hand. "Just lend me your baton for a moment, and allow me on the podium." Then, turning to the orchestra, "Let's begin again."

The baton swept into motion, and the sound that came out of the orchestra had vibrancy and spirit unlike anything the student had achieved. The maestro stopped after only about thirty seconds and the players shuffled their feet.

The student conductor seemed amazed.

"Now let's consider," the maestro said, returning the student's baton, "what just happened. Do you think they played that way because I have gray hair, or because they think I have some kind of authority over them?" The answer was plain from the shaking heads in the orchestra. "There is really only one fundamental difference between what you did and what I did. Your conducting happens in parallel with the orchestra, whereas I commit to what they haven't yet played.

"A leader must commit to that which *has not yet happened*. Otherwise you are not really leading; in fact, you are actually following. It feels very comfortable and right to do all those beautiful gestures at the same time as the music is happening, but it has no effect whatsoever on the playing. To affect the orchestra's playing, you must prehear the music that they are *about* to play. That's what I did, and that was the only reason you heard such a different sound. So now, you try," he concluded, and he backed off the podium.

The student raised his baton and began. No more than fifteen seconds went by before the maestro interrupted.

"No," he said. "It's the same as before. Live the music they are about to play. Use your baton to show what is coming next."

He began again, and this time everyone felt the difference. It was remarkable to me that such a fundamental change could be affected by a matter of such subtle timing.

The student seemed to be more shocked than anyone else. "That's such a strange feeling!" he exclaimed.

"Yes, it is," agreed the maestro. "It's almost counterintuitive. What feels right is to be *with* the orchestra, but that is not leading. What feels uncomfortable is to lead, which actually means that the baton is not in the same time zone as the orchestra's playing."

The student was nodding agreement with this new idea.

"And furthermore," the maestro said, "how do you decide what gestures to make with the baton? It is the conductor's aural image, prehearing how the orchestra might sound, that dictates how the arm should move. So the conductor's imagination is in one time zone, the baton in the next, and the orchestra's sound in the third. And the conductor must coordinate it all!"

"He must be in three time zones, simultaneously?"

"Right."

"But how is that possible?" asked the student in disbelief.

"Have you ever watched a broadcast from the United Nations? Think of the job that the simultaneous translators are doing. While following the speaker's thoughts in one language they are speaking the same thoughts a moment later in another language. Yet while spinning out the idea in the second language they are still listening to what the speaker has gone on to say. It's quite a feat.

"Now, in the case of the translators, their thoughts are lagging behind the action of the speaker. In the case of a conductor, his thoughts are anticipating the playing of the orchestra. It is only in anticipating, and committing to what will happen next, that any leadership can take place."

"What happens if the conductor isn't anticipating or committing to what will happen next?"

"Then his baton will have no effect whatsoever on the orchestra, and they will start to ignore him. "

"Is that what happened with me?"

"Think about it," he said, inviting the student to step down, indicating that his lesson was over. "If the conducting is merely affirming what the players are already doing, it amounts to little more than cheerleading. With so much that you have to offer, you owe the professionals whom you lead more than that."

"Thank you, Maestro."

By now I had a pit in my stomach. How could I have missed the boat so completely? I had focused this morning's meeting primarily on fixing *past* mistakes. I hadn't even considered that my imagination could live in the *future*—a future that could be shaped by my capacity to conceive it in vivid detail. The act of envisioning our company—not as it is today, but as it needs to be to meet the challenges of the future—could have a profound impact on what we can actually achieve.

Here I was, impatiently waiting for my team to engage with this new future reality when I wasn't willing to do so myself. I had no idea that withholding my own commitment to the vision was preventing my people from taking the kind of bold, confident action we desperately needed. It was all very well that I was encouraging them to work together more efficiently, but how far could that take us if there was still doubt about what, exactly, they were working toward.

My despondency about my own failings suddenly gave way to a buoyant optimism. Maybe a business leader like me is capable of a sort of sorcery, just like a conductor. The secret lies in the implausible act of existing in several time zones simultaneously, some of them concretely real and others as amorphous and weightless as a mere possibility. What energizes people is the leader's act of committing to what is possible.

Sharing the Maestro's Lessons

IT TOOK A FEW MORE MONTHS BEFORE I'D DIGESTED THE maestro's lessons enough to affect the behavior of my leadership team in a lasting way. But soon enough I began to notice that there was a new level of engagement and energy.

Executives were taking more ownership of the entire company, not just the division that they led. During our meetings people were now in the habit of discussing their issues together rather than protecting their territory. We had learned not to spend our time on local, technical problems that could be delegated to a single department. But when an issue was caused by a more systemic failure, spanning company boundaries, the leadership team had gotten quite skilled at solving it collaboratively.

Breakdowns in the flow of information or material continued, of course. But when confronted with a problem, my leaders had developed the collective discipline to replace knee-jerk reactions and their impulse to find quick fixes with curiosity about analyzing the entire system. Instead of applying a patch, they were learning how to awaken a larger awareness of the problem within their own teams so that a solution could be found collectively.

They had gotten very clever about locating the exact place

to apply leverage, the right trim tab, so that the company or their department could adjust its course efficiently. And only when absolutely necessary did they have to dole out punishment, assign blame, or employ coercive tactics to guide and correct their employees.

For my part, I had learned the surprising power of listening: how it inspires lively and productive discussion. I had long since jettisoned the misguided idea that my employees would perceive an open ear and inquisitive mind as signs of weakness or uncertainty. Instead I found that they stimulated more flexibility and creativity in the team. And by listening from many different time zones, as the maestro taught me, I was able to point our debates away from the rehashing of old grievances and toward a future that was worth working for.

All of these changes and many more enabled the leadership team to align around a vision and strategy that we believed was right for a volatile and unpredictable business environment. This was a major achievement, of course, but it was only a beginning. Now it was time for the entire organization to implement the strategy.

It had taken the leadership team months to get used to routinely collaborating across boundaries, sharing information and thinking about the company's big picture. We didn't have the luxury of another half year to bring the rest of the organization along, so we started talking about organizing an off-site conference for the top 250 leaders in the company.

Of course, everyone would have to come away from this meeting with a crystal-clear understanding of our new strategy and vision. But that was not enough. When a strategy hits the ground, those implementing it need to feel confident in modifying and adapting it to the terrain on which it will run. We couldn't afford a "do what you're told" mentality, or a "follow the instructions" mind-set.

The conference needed to enroll those who did the everyday work in a partnership: everyone, no matter at what level, would be a co-creator of our newly collaborative, flexible, fast, accurate, and reliable organization. Above all, I wanted them to walk away from the conference with a vivid impression, a real taste of how it would feel to operate that way.

Our objective was clear, but I still had moments of doubt. It had taken months to instill those attitudes in the executive team. How could we do it for the rest of the organization in just one conference? I'd never been to an off-site event that accomplished anything like that, or liberated that kind of feeling and energy. So I started to ask myself how I had learned these lessons. What had helped me to develop and take on these new behaviors?

It didn't take much reflection to realize that it was my experience inside the orchestra that had made the greatest impact. But I struggled with the question of how to help my people learn in a similar way. Taking them all to a concert was clearly not the answer. No, I had been allowed to have a remarkable and uncommon learning experience, and I could not think of a way to translate it to my organization.

Then, like the proverbial lightning bolt, it hit me. Why not give the participants at the conference *exactly* the same experience I'd had! Why not seat them inside the orchestra, and let the conductor show them what I had seen. My mind was already spinning with ideas, but I knew my first task just might be the hardest. I had to convince the maestro.

As the conductor listened to me describe my idea, his face was very uncharacteristically blank. He was an exceptional listener, with a very creative mind. Still, he could not grasp my picture of the conference.

"Tell me," he said, before asking with the utmost candor, "is this a joke?"

What I was asking of him was unlike anything that he had ever contemplated, but I persisted in explaining how it would work. I knew the major concepts and ideas I wanted to stress at the conference. I had seen each of these in action from my chair in the orchestra. It was no easy task to persuade him. But at last he said, "Well, I must say, this is quite an idea of yours. I'm not sure that I'm up to it."

I assured him that I was totally convinced he could carry it off. He had already demonstrated that he could make all of these issues come alive to me!

"Maestro," I said, "you will be doing far more than just helping my company. When I came to my first rehearsal I had no understanding about classical music. To be honest with you, I was afraid of it!"

He scoffed at the idea.

"No, it's true! But over the weeks I have developed a profound connection with the music. I will never hear another concert in the way I used to. By agreeing to do this you will give birth to a new class of music lovers."

Now he looked at me with curiosity.

"You taught me to hear. You've made a lifelong concertgoer out of me. If you work with me on this project you will have a fresh infusion of people coming to your performances, I am certain of it. Who knows, some may even want to serve on the orchestra's board of directors. Please consider what an opportunity this is for both of us."

He stared off into the distance, as I had many times seen him do when he was imagining a piece of music. "It would require me to stitch together all the educational programs I've ever designed: private teaching, conservatory teaching, children's concerts, speeches that I've given." He looked directly at me. "I'm beginning to see how this could be done."

He tapped his fingertips together a few times, and then brought them to his lips. "Give me some time to think about this."

It was a strange feeling for me when the conductor walked into the conference room at my office. So many times while sitting around this table I had recalled the lessons I'd learned in his dressing room or in my chairs among the players. Now he was actually here, a maestro who routinely stands at the nerve center of an orchestra, sitting at the nerve center of a business organization whose aim is making money.

Through a great accident he had come into my life at this pivotal time, and for me the line separating music and business had not only been blurred, it had completely dissolved. I am a businessman. That's the domain in which I live. Yet thinking about business now often brought music to my mind. And when I thought about my understanding of an orchestra, those images now often suggested business analogies to me.

Some may view these two worlds as incongruous, but central to both business and music is the human capacity for communicating, working together, and self-actualization. Through no credit to myself I stumbled on the use of this metaphor, and it pointed the way toward endless possibilities for me and my team. Now I had a chance to share this new way of looking at our work with the rest of my company. I couldn't even remember the last time I had been so excited about anything at work.

I shook hands with the conductor and welcomed him into my office, and we took a seat at the table. After we got settled in he said, "So please help me understand how you see this working."

"I'd like to give you some background about the company and the conference, and then tell you specifically what my goals are for your session. You can interrupt me at any time to clarify if something is not clear. Agreed?"

He nodded his assent.

I began by telling him about the accelerating changes in our business environment. The company was like a boat with slow leaks, and though it was urgent to repair the leaks and right the ship, that wasn't nearly enough. We had to chart a new course through rough and dangerous seas. This course was our business vision, which was based on a new kind of relationship with our customers and business partners. By working together as a single interdependent system we could offer our customers the products and services they needed at lower costs.

"But it all depends on the entire company operating with the same communication and alignment skills that I saw demonstrated in the orchestra. That's what I want to get across," I concluded.

"Which skills are you talking about? You sat in on quite a few rehearsals. What did you see that impressed you?"

I told him about the many lessons I learned from the orchestra and him: the orchestra's rapid and coordinated response to his direction; how he led them to team up with players whose work was being done beyond earshot; the role of a conductor in creating a vision that inspires his team and creates a sense of community.

As I spoke he feverishly scribbled notes on a legal pad from the table. When I was done he continued to write for a few moments and then looked up. "Well, you've been a very attentive student."

"I don't think so. I think that you are an unusually gifted teacher, and you will provide us with an amazing competitive advantage."

We discussed how all of these messages might be conveyed. The conductor was very concerned about logistical issues regarding the hotel ballroom where the orchestra session would take place: the square footage, the lighting, the room setup, microphones for him and for participants to speak into, runners to swiftly deliver microphones to wherever they were necessary. His attentiveness to this level of detail revealed a factor that I should have noted, but had escaped me until that very moment. He was a *performer*. His career was made standing in front of orchestras and audiences, almost always as the center of attention. He knew how to make his communication dramatic. He knew how to create an atmosphere and how important it is to do so.

It was commonplace for him to devote considerable attention to the small details that most people fail to notice, but whose combined effect is a memorable and moving experience. The same care that he devoted to the shaping of a phrase or the pacing of a crescendo he now lavished on the exact height of his podium and the placement of every single chair, for both musicians and participants.

When he left my office I found it difficult to contain my excitement and anticipation about how he was going to design this lesson. But nothing in my highest expectations could prepare me for what actually happened.

The Session

IN MID-JULY NEARLY 250 PEOPLE FROM MY ORGANIZA-
tion filled the conference rooms at a nearby hotel for a three-
day meeting. These were the leaders who would take our new
strategy back to the rest of the company and weave it into the
fabric of our business.

We had organized quite a full agenda, with many different
learning events to introduce them to the new goals, and I was
gratified to see so many members of my own leadership team
rising to the occasion. They were delivering speeches, facilitating
discussions, or simply disseminating the spirit of our initiative.

No one knew anything about the orchestra session except
the leadership team; and nobody, including me, knew exactly
what it would be like. The agenda simply read, "Leadership
Exercise—Main Ballroom."

The session was scheduled exactly midway through the conference, on the afternoon of the second day. While our people
were engaged in small discussion groups throughout the conference center, the main ballroom had been set up for the orchestra. I was burning with curiosity, and stuck my head in to
see how the conductor had prepared the room.

It looked like a large amphitheater, with the podium at the
focal point. The traditional orchestra setup was spread out to

fill the entire ballroom, leaving space for 250 chairs interspersed throughout the sections. Care had been taken to place each participant as close to a player as possible. Musicians had begun to arrive, and some were already warming up.

"The orchestra has to learn how to play in such a strange setup," the maestro had explained to me. "We'll need almost an hour of rehearsal just to locate one another's sound in this huge space, and to make whatever adjustments are necessary."

Curious as I was, I couldn't linger because I was scheduled to preside over a discussion in another part of the hotel about how the new strategy would affect people and their jobs. So when the time arrived and all 250 of us headed toward the ballroom en masse, I was pretty much in the same boat as everyone else. I was very nervous about whether or not this would succeed, but I still enjoyed others' expressions of surprise as we entered the brightly lit room and were simply asked to take any seat where there was no music stand.

One of my objectives in planning this conference went far beyond announcing our new business model. I hoped to stimulate fresh and creative thinking on the spot. I didn't want these leaders to feel like passive participants in a massive change. They needed to understand that our strategy was a living organism and that I was inviting them—in fact, I *expected* them— to participate in its continuing evolution. I needed them to own this process in the same way that the leadership team had come to own it. And I was counting on this session with the orchestra to jolt them out of complacency and routine thought patterns.

As the room filled up, musicians dressed in full concert attire began to file in. They seemed as taken aback as my people did. It was only later that I learned that while the conductor had rehearsed the music, he had not said a single word about what would happen during the session. The musicians knew only where to start playing. That was all.

Once everyone had found their seats around the ballroom, the concertmaster stood up and tuned the orchestra. The participants grew quiet and expectant. Then I stepped forward and read a simple introduction of the conductor and orchestra. To polite applause the maestro ascended the taller-than-normal podium and began to conduct. I was in a good position to watch my people as their eyes wandered about the room and they craned their necks to look at something they had heard but couldn't quite see. When the piece came to its rousing conclusion they burst into applause, and the session was launched.

In his disarmingly natural way the conductor welcomed us all inside the orchestra. "What if," he asked, "through an act of your imagination you could transform this orchestra into more than just a musical ensemble. Suppose it were also a state-of-the-art twenty-first-century information organization, with that certain something that we're all looking for?" He paused. "A competitive advantage.

"What if this superiority derived from certain skills that abound in the orchestra: the ability to work in teams, to communicate effectively and rapidly, to exercise leadership at all levels, and to align around a vision so that the entire organization speaks with one voice? And suppose you were here as spies, with the assignment to pirate as much as you could; to try to transplant these skills into your own professional life. In fact, that's your assignment this afternoon."

He directed the orchestra to a new passage, and as the musicians were turning the pages to find the right spot he revealed to us that this entire presentation was unscripted. Only the music had been rehearsed, but the presentation was spontaneous. This brought some knowing smiles to the faces of the musicians, which made it clear to all that he was speaking the truth.

After the orchestra played the second passage, the conductor

asked the first violins to stand. I saw expressions of mild dis-
comfort and confusion on the violinists' faces as they raised
their music stands and stood up.

To the rest of us the conductor said, "Now, with your mind's
eye, make everything in the room disappear, except for the
bows in these violinists' hands." He waited for a moment before
going on, as if giving us all time to follow his direction. "And
now, carefully watch those bows as they play this passage."

I could feel how everyone's attention was riveted as the violinists prepared to play. Then the bows sprang into action. They
all moved in exactly the same direction with split-second timing. It was delightful to notice how the bows changed their
angles in such perfect synchronicity. They looked like identical
parts of an enormous, well-oiled, complicated machine, all
driven by the same motor. When the violinists stopped, the
conductor made that very same observation. Yet, he remarked,
the unison of their movements was not the result of a single
engine, but rather of a group of people, each of whom was
simply making very good and extremely timely decisions.

To prove this, he turned toward the violinists and said,
"Now suppose, ladies and gentlemen, that for some strange
reason you decide that you're tired of being part of the herd." I
could see smiles immediately cross the violinists' faces, and hear
their repressed sniggers. "Today, you decide, I'm going to be an
individual. I know, as part of this violin section, I must play together with my colleagues. But I'm going to make up my own
bowings. When I finish, I want to feel that 'I did it *my* way.'"

Now there was open laughter from my people, for whom
this exercise must have hit the funny bone. Their curiosity was
even more piqued than before as the violinists once again raised
their instruments and began to play. What a hodgepodge of
contradictory motions, each bow going its own way. Yet the
music was not discordant or objectionable. Indeed, it still

sounded like it was made by professional musicians, but the attention to detail and a special expressive power was lost to the music. When they stopped playing, both musicians and executives shared a spontaneous, playful moment.

"Now," the conductor's voice rang out over the merriment and wisecracks, "you've just heard a fine example of what happens when every individual on the team is performing extremely well, but the teamwork is deficient."

He grabbed a microphone stationed on his podium and walked toward the violinists, who had by now sat down. Handing the mike to a clearly unsuspecting musician, he asked, "What skills does it require to play the way you did at first? What do you have to be capable of doing?"

"Well"—she hesitated, as if she had never considered this question before—"first you have to decide that you're willing to go along with the rest." She reflected still more. "Then you have to listen very carefully to your colleagues, and find the way that you can contribute to the whole."

"Why would anyone willingly decide to 'go along,' as you say? Wasn't it more fun to do it your own way?"

"No, no," she answered without hesitation. "It was terrible! I didn't feel the support of people around me, and I was no longer sure how to play. You see, we build off of one another's energy. When you have a group that's well disciplined in teamwork, it liberates you to do your best. And then you feel like you're contributing to something that's very worthwhile. Often, as an orchestra, we can rise to a level that's much higher than I could achieve as an individual. So when the orchestra plays really well I feel privileged to be part of it, and I want to contribute."

"Thank you very much," he said softly, acknowledging the magnitude of what she had just expressed, as he took the microphone back to the podium.

I was amazed at how such a simple demonstration could have

such a profound and moving effect on my people. Had I tried to teach the same lesson myself it would have sounded trite and tiresome, like a worn-out platitude. But on the lips of a musician in this unfamiliar context, the value of giving yourself over to the greater mission was meaningful to all the leaders in the room.

The conductor wandered to the perimeter of the room, and was now selecting an employee who was quite far from his podium. He led her on a zigzag path through the crowded orchestra until she was standing on the podium with him. "The reason I chose you, and the only reason, is because you were so very far away from the podium. Come to think of it," he quipped, "aren't there always some offices that feel quite removed from the center of the action: where you feel like you're the last one to find out what's going on?" A laugh of recognition rippled spontaneously through the entire group.

"Well, Pamela," he gently explained, noticing her name tag, "your job is to listen to this passage that you've already heard a few times, and just compare how it sounds, feels, and looks from up here." The orchestra played, and I saw Pamela's eyes darting about. She was indeed having the experience that I'd only imagined having weeks ago, when I stood on the podium in the empty concert hall.

"So, Pamela, what's your report?"

"It's so different up here!"

"What do you mean?"

"Well . . ." She collected her thoughts, clearly trying to put into words something that defied description. "It's so vibrant here. You can hear everything!"

"And what about from your chair?"

"Well, I was near . . . What are those instruments called? Oh yes, French horns, and that was all that I could hear."

"And?"

"It was great. It was glorious. But it was all French horn."

"Did you hear the horns from up here on the podium?"

"Oh yes! But they were so beautifully mixed with everything else. I could hear the strings from up here."

"And did you hear the woodwinds, too?"

"Yes."

"And from your chair?"

"Only French horns," she said with an innocent smile, and there was good-hearted laughter around the room, sparked by Pamela's guileless responses.

"Now let's all consider why this is important," he said, bringing a focus and purpose to what had seemed like just fun. "It's no accident that you're hearing all of the instruments from here," he said, pointing to the podium. "The entire room is set up to make this place special. This is the podium, and it's the place to which all information flows. From here you get a strategic view of the orchestra, you hear all the activity, and the sounds of one instrument don't eclipse another. That's what the podium is about.

"But orchestras aren't the only organizations that have them. Every organization that has to work in a coordinated way has at least one podium, and probably many. That is where we place the leader. I know that each of you is in this room today because you play a leadership role at your company. With respect to the people who are accountable to you, you are on a podium." I could see that there were lots of nodding heads.

"Let's say, Pamela, that you need to get an activity coordinated, and it requires the involvement of one person from the string section, and another from the horns. From up here, that's no sweat. You hear them both clearly and can clearly see how they can sound together. So you tell them to get coordinated. But you start to lose patience with them when they fail again and again. Because from up *here* you don't see a problem. But from the horn chair, this musician has no idea what you're ask-ing for because he can't hear it! There is an inevitable commu-nications gap between the podium and the chair.

"Now, when I was a young and foolish conductor I thought this was the musicians' problem. No wonder I caused such stress and accomplished so little then! Now, with my gray hair, I understand that it falls to the person in the leadership position to stretch his or her imagination to include not only the reality from the podium, but also that from the chair.

"Now, Pamela, look longingly at your old chair, way off in the distance."

She smiled at his playfulness.

"Do you see it? Just for now, remember what the sound was like there."

I could see on Pamela's face that she was really thinking; and these were not thoughts that she had had before. As I scanned the room I saw that look on many people's faces: the dawning of a fresh thought.

"Now, really think like a conductor," he urged her. "Let your eyes roam around the room, and try to imagine what the sound would be like from each chair."

The room was absolutely silent, all eyes on Pamela.

"It gives you some appreciation," he said, "of what it takes to get people to coordinate their activities, and to be aware of one another. It shows how much the leader, with her privileged point of view from the podium, can help people in the chairs to make the right connections."

She nodded her head.

"Now here's your next assignment: in a moment you'll fi-nally return to your chair. But when you're there, try to re-member as much as you can about what it's like up here. You will be able to capture the big picture, even if your ears can't actually hear it."

"How do I do that, if I can't hear it?"

"You use the memory of what you heard up here, and you use your imagination. Because that is the amazing teamwork skill the musicians have. Regardless of where they sit, they always think of the big picture."

She nodded in understanding and stepped down from the podium. The applause that accompanied Pamela on her way back to her chair was warm and openhearted. I noticed that the musicians were applauding, too. I was stunned at how the conductor had turned the room into a community in just twenty minutes!

"Now," he said, waiting for the room to settle down, "another aspect of the orchestra's amazing teamwork is their ability to tune to one another. You see, we have all become quite expert at meticulously adhering to the same standard. But what if that were not so? What if we had warring factions within our ranks that insisted upon the superiority of their way?"

I could see where the conductor was going now, and it delighted me to see him translate one of our most acute cultural issues into an experiential exercise.

"To fully understand this, I have to ask the musicians to do something that will be very loathsome to them. So," he said, addressing the principal oboe, "would you offer to the woodwinds and brass a nice A that is just a quarter tone lower than our normal A 440."

This remark was met by a chorus of groans from the wind players. I understood why. One of the horn players had once explained to me that orchestras tune to A at a pitch of 440 vibrations per second. The instruments are built to this standard. Now the conductor was asking the brass and woodwinds to play against the nature of their instruments. I could read the players' body language, and they were very uncomfortable and apprehensive. The oboe played the new A, and the wind players winced.

"Now, let's hear only those who have retuned."

The brass and woodwinds played the passage we had heard throughout the session. At first it was quite sour, but within half a minute it sounded like the dust had settled, and their professional polish had returned. "Very good!" he complimented them.

"Ladies and gentlemen," he said to my people, "you have just had the rare opportunity to witness an organization as it adapts to new and uncomfortable circumstances. It was a challenge, but they persevered and overcame the hardship. Now," he said, turning his attention to the strings, who seemed to have found this exercise rather amusing, "what if the strings play on their own standard while the woodwinds and brass play on theirs? What would that sound like?"

The musicians groused in mock protest. When they played, the effect was astonishing! It sounded like my daughter's high school orchestra—that unforgettable sour sound of struggling music students.

There was general levity when they stopped, but the conductor did not encourage it.

"This is the sound of an organization that can't agree on the standards and processes to which it will adhere. The remarkable thing here," he exclaimed with special emphasis, "is that every single musician was doing an outstanding, professional job. The problem was not with the individuals; it was with the organization's inability to resolve its differences."

There was no longer any chuckling in the room. I was fascinated by the atmosphere he had created. Here were my people, witnessing a striking and memorable demonstration of one of their most unproductive dysfunctions, and yet nobody was feeling defensive. Instead they were riveted, leaning forward in their chairs, eager to hear more.

"Now, in the orchestra we pride ourselves on our strict adherence to a single pitch standard. It's a choice that we all willingly make; it's the price one pays in order to play in tune. So," he said to the oboist, "would you please restore us all to the same A?"

The orchestra tuned. It was a sound I'd heard hundreds of times in movies, at concerts, and at the rehearsals, yet it had never had the significance that it had at that moment. The musicians were aligning around a norm, each player making sure that his or her own behavior would support that norm.

When they were ready, the maestro said, "Now what will it sound like when every single musician is dedicated to upholding that standard, making every C the same, regardless of who plays it; every G the same? What would that sound like?"

He raised his baton, and out came a sound that was not only free of its former blemishes, it was placid and transparent, as if muddy silt had finally settled, and you could now see with crystal clarity to the very bottom of a riverbed. This sound had such a feeling of serenity and repose that nobody could escape its spell.

When the excerpt was finished there was a moment of stillness in the room, followed by generous applause. The demonstration had hit its mark. But the conductor wasn't finished with the issue of playing in tune. He walked out into the orchestra and handed the microphone to the principal flutist. She was obviously taken aback and instantly colored.

"How did you do that?" he inquired. "How did you create that amazing atmosphere just now?"

"Well . . ." she hesitated, as if not knowing at all how to explain what had just happened. "First of all, we all tuned to the same A. That was helpful."

The room lit up with laughter.

"And then we all listened very attentively."

"When you're a professional, it must be pretty easy to play in tune, right?"

She seemed very surprised by the question. "Oh no," she shot back. "It's very difficult!"

"Why? I mean, you're all extremely accomplished. There are no weak links here. How could it still be difficult?"

"Well, even when you're very good at what you do, problems of agreement still come up."

"I know it's not realistic to attach numbers to an intuitive mental process, but just for discussion's sake, what percentage of your attention would you say goes to playing in tune?"

She thought about this for a moment. "Maybe anywhere from seventy-five to one hundred percent." There was a reaction of surprise in the room.

"That much?" he said.

"Yes. It's our major preoccupation. You see, it doesn't matter how good you sound if you don't match the others who are playing with you."

"So what do you have to do, to match?"

"We listen to one another very carefully, in great detail. We're all ready to adjust at any moment, and we do make adjustments constantly."

"But suppose you're right? Suppose you know that you're in tune. Can't you ask the others to adjust to you?"

She laughed at this notion. "There is no such thing as being right. It's like, which would you rather, being right or sounding in tune? Sounding in tune is about everyone valuing the collective sound as the highest priority."

"And what happens when you have a player who knows with certainty that he's right?"

"It's hell!"

Again, her reactions elicited laughter from the group.

"It's just such a chore. You can't get things to match; so then you try diplomacy, but that probably won't work either. A musician who's pigheaded about intonation is a curse for an orchestra. Fortunately, it rarely happens."

"Why not?"

"Because part of being an excellent player is your ability, desire, and interest in adjusting. It's almost on the same level as playing the right notes."

"Thank you very much," he said, taking the microphone from her hand as the entire room offered a round of spontaneous applause.

I didn't have to wonder whether my more recalcitrant people were listening. Everyone was listening! And I could tell by the pensive expressions I saw everywhere in the room that people were challenging themselves, wondering if they could be this kind of professional.

The conductor had been boasting quite a bit about the musicians' proficiency in teamwork, communication, and alignment. That was, after all, the skill set that gave them their "competitive advantage." At one point he said that the orchestra had such an abundance of this expertise that, as they would now demonstrate, they were perfectly capable of playing beautifully without anyone on the podium. Then, without uttering another word, he walked off the podium and stood in one of the corners of the room, his back turned to everyone.

I wished that I could have made a slow-motion video of what happened next. In a matter of seconds the entire organization was redefining itself, establishing new leadership roles, clearing new channels for communication, and it was all done without a single word or gesture. All this tacit understanding was conveyed exclusively through eye contact.

I focused my attention on the concertmaster who was waiting for the orchestra's concentration to build. He gave a motion with his violin and his bow that looked like he was taking a big breath. Instantly I heard the sound of all the wind players breathing in. Then came the sound from all over the room, beginning at precisely the same split second, without a trace of tentativeness or hesitation.

With the movements of their instruments the musicians seemed to be sending signals to each other. On their faces I saw expressions of heightened alertness as the room filled with a sound that was beautifully blended and balanced.

From every corner of the room my employees were wearing expressions of great curiosity. Some even looked skeptical, as if they were trying to figure out the gimmick. But by the end of the passage they must have been convinced that this demonstration of spontaneous collaboration across the entire orchestra was authentic, because their applause was especially warm and generous.

The conductor returned to the podium and remained silent, as if in thought, for a few moments.

"This is a very challenging demonstration for a conductor," he said with a hint of entreaty in his voice. This evoked gleeful laughter, especially from the musicians.

"Really," he went on, once the merriment had died down. "If the orchestra can do this without anyone on the podium, don't you think that raises some uncomfortable questions for me?" Laughter again.

"What is the value added by this?" he asked, raising his baton. "And this is a question every conductor ought to ask himself frequently. I wonder if there is merit in an executive asking the same question." The laughter had ceased.

"After all, this oversized toothpick I'm holding in my right hand," he said, indicating his baton, "is not a musical instrument. It creates no sound." He paused. "What's it good for, anyway?"

I could have heard a pin drop in the room as the conductor waited for his questions to sink in and for the participants to draw their own conclusions about the leadership tools that they wielded. He went on, "You know, talk is cheap. If we're going to consider whether the baton adds value, there's only one way to find out."

He raised his arms, and the orchestra understood that they were going to play while he conducted once again. Then he led them through the very same passage that they had just played without him. The difference was remarkable. As I looked around the room I saw that there was openness on my people's faces, as if they were hearing an oracle speak some long-sought truth. When the passage was over the room burst into its warmest applause yet.

"I want you to understand," the maestro said to his musicians, "that this applause was for you. It was your playing that moved them. Am I right, Doris?" he said as he picked his way through the chairs and handed the microphone to an executive who seemed to have been particularly moved.

"Oh my," was all she could say. "That was so beautiful."

"It was beautiful before, wasn't it?" he countered.

"You mean when they did it without you?"

"Yes."

"Yes, it was beautiful. But there was something else this last time."

"You heard the very same notes, right?"

"Yes. But there was soul in it. I don't know how else to describe it."

"Did it make much of a difference?"

"Oh my God, yes! It made all the difference in the world!"

"Thank you," he said kindly, taking the microphone and returning to the podium.

"All of you know that there are moments when we leaders try to change things. We announce an initiative, we explain it, we take questions, we send out reminders. Then six months later nothing has changed.

"It's very tempting to believe that leadership is a fiction: that leadership doesn't really work. We rationalize by saying, 'Just get good people together and let them do their work.' But if you were in this room just now, there is no longer any way that you can deny what you saw and heard. Leadership doesn't make a small difference. As Doris remarked, it makes all the difference in the world. Though the notes were the same, there was a oneness, a focus, an alignment that took place, and everyone knew it.

"If you're a leader, if you stand on a podium, if you hold in your hand a baton, then it falls on your shoulders to make the remarkable happen. You mustn't settle for a series of satisfactory transactions. You *can* elevate your team to heights beyond their wildest imagination. Now that you have been in this room and seen this happen you can never quite let yourself off the hook in the same way again."

The session ended with a rousing performance of the entire piece of music. To everyone's delight, the conductor had invited people to choose a new location in the room from which to hear it. Many people stepped up onto the podium, surrounding him, and listened from there. After the final chord had sounded the musicians were cheered as heroes.

Maestro

THE ORCHESTRA SESSION CREATED QUITE A BUZZ THROUGH-
out the rest of the conference. The next day the discussions and
general meetings were charged with an energy that I'd never
seen before. Still more unprecedented was the openness of the
conversations and general willingness to consider other points
of view. Some people who had always struck me as intransigent
and headstrong came up to me and commented warmly about
their experience inside the orchestra.

I had watched carefully as people entered the ballroom just
before the orchestra session began. I noticed that almost everyone had walked in grouped by department. That was not surprising; they work side by side every day, and they share a
common background, training, and even a unique technical
language. But the unexpected configuration of the room, with
seats sprinkled willy-nilly throughout the orchestra, made it
impossible for people to keep their groups intact. After the session was over, however, I saw that people left the room in lively
spontaneous conversation with new colleagues from other
departments.

Of course the musicians sit in silos, too: the brass with the
brass, the strings with the strings. But when they play the silos
dissolve. The tone of one player blends with another, and you

can no more take the sound apart than you can separate oil paints that have been mixed and blended on a canvas.

When the sounds combine it creates harmony, and I think it was the orchestra's harmony that overwhelmed us. It actually changed how we conceived of our organization, and what we believed we could make of it. Certainly the conductor had not asked us to think that way. We just discovered it for ourselves. And when an entire workforce gets truly fascinated by a new-found capability, they will very likely make it their own.

I invited the conductor out for lunch about two weeks after the conference. I wanted to thank him and let him know how much he and his orchestra had given us. But I had also begun to notice a hazy cloud of doubt gathering around the sunny feelings I'd been enjoying since the session. Something that I couldn't put my finger on was beginning to trouble me, and I wanted to talk to the maestro about it.

It was true that the offsite had generated such an optimistic feeling in all of us. But I'd been back in the day-to-day realities of running the company since then, and my hopefulness was beginning to fade. These were difficult times, and it was hard to keep up with the fast-breaking developments on almost every front.

The lessons I'd learned in the orchestra, and that I'd shared with my employees at the conference, had definitely helped me and my company to face these challenges. But behind every-thing I learned from the maestro was the idea that as a leader I must guide the team by holding my vision in mind at all times.

He said that his every gesture, every word, even every facial expression was connected to his vision, which lived in his imagination in luminescent clarity. Well, in real life it's just not that simple. I was surprised by the flash of frustration that this thought provoked in me. Clearly I was rebelling against something, but I couldn't really understand my strong reaction until the middle of our lunch.

When we sat down at our table I took great pleasure in expressing my profound gratitude to him. He seemed to enjoy hearing any number of anecdotes about the impact his presentation had had on my people. Then suddenly I knew what had been bothering me. "You know, there's one thing I have to say. I don't think I can agree with your premise about vision."

He stopped eating and looked at me with intense curiosity. "Tell me more," he invited.

"Well, it's one thing to speak of vision when you're conducting a symphony that was composed in the 1840s, and whose notes haven't changed since Mendelssohn jotted them down on paper. You can study that same score today and examine every pristine note in full knowledge that when you get to the rehearsal the musicians are going to be playing exactly the same notes that you studied.

"Yes," he replied, "that is true."

"Well, it's not true for me, or for anyone who's running a company these days. It feels like the rules by which we play the game of business are being rewritten every time we blink. How can you ever hold to a vision when the ground is constantly shifting underneath you? How can you believe in a vision when there are so many notes being played that you can't possibly be aware of what they are?"

He could see that I wasn't finished. "Please go on," he urged me.

"We business leaders can't even conceive of the multifarious operations that tens of thousands of employees perform every day to achieve our goals. But a conductor has every single note in front of him in his score. You just can't compare the two."

As soon as these words had passed my lips I wished that I had not spoken so candidly. After all, the conductor had never claimed that his advice was about running a business. He had only shared the inner workings of what he and his musicians do. I was afraid that I'd blamed him for my own frustrations at work. But the receptive expression on his face quickly put me at ease.

"This is a very good point you've made. I want to think about it."

After a few moments he spoke again. "You've helped me to understand some of the very daunting challenges that a leader like you faces. Yes, it is very different from what we conductors do. I could most certainly never do your job. So I was just asking myself whether I've done you and the people in your company a disservice by inviting you into my world. Have I misled you?"

He fell silent again. I knew him well enough now to realize that he was still processing this question, and was not going to give a flippant answer. So I sat back and waited.

"You know," he began again, "there's a lot of misunderstanding about the kind of music I conduct. Many people think that, because we classical musicians read our music and always play a given piece with exactly the same notes, that we are not as creative or spontaneous as, say, jazz musicians, who play by ear and improvise on the spot. But that's a fallacy. It's a mistake to believe that the music resides in the notes. The notes are essential. As you point out, they are what the composer puts down on paper. But all of those notes are like the network of wires that make up a complicated electrical circuit. Once the circuitry has been laid and connected there still has to be electricity generated to flow through those wires to make anything happen."

"But you talk about notes all the time in rehearsal," I protested. "Should they be long or short, connected or detached, loud or soft, foreground or background . . ."

"Yes, yes," he interrupted me, smiling, "you're right. The circuitry also must be perfectly laid, or even the most powerful electric current will go nowhere. But it is possible, even commonplace, that all the notes are executed flawlessly and you still have none of the actual music."

"How's that?" I asked. "I don't see it."

He closed his eyes in thought for a moment. "Well, you probably don't know the *Theresa* Mass by Haydn."

I shook my head.

"Most music lovers don't know it—it's not performed very often—but I think it's one of Haydn's most inspired works, written at the very height of his creative powers. I was once rehearsing it with an excellent chorus of amateur singers. The second movement is the Credo, whose text in effect lists the tenets of the Catholic faith—all of the beliefs.

"During the rehearsal the chorus was singing it accurately, in tune, with good rhythm. The tempo was right. Yet the music was totally devoid of spirit, as if they were merely following instructions. The notes were there, but none of the music. I'd tried giving all kinds of musical directions, to no avail."

"So what did you do?"

"Finally I asked the chorus to imagine the following scenario. We are living in a country that has suffered under a repressive foreign military occupation for decades. The singing of our national anthem has been harshly suppressed. Everybody still knows the tune and the words, but they haven't been heard for as long as anyone can remember. Then comes the glorious liberation day. Tyranny is overthrown and we all rush out into the public square. And spontaneously we break into song. Nobody knows who started it. Nobody is leading it. We look around the square and on everyone's lips are the same words that our grandparents and great-grandparents had grown up singing. What would that be like? How would it sound?"

"And what did it sound like?"

"For the first time it sounded like the piece was about *belief.* Not notes, but *conviction*—a mass of people manifesting the strongest bond holding them together, their common belief. If Haydn's Credo is sung without that feeling, then it's just not what he composed, even if every single note is perfect."

"I understand. You generated the current that flowed through those notes," I agreed.

"No, not quite. The singers generated the current. I created the image that inspired them to do that. And," he said, looking straight into my eyes, "there was no instruction in the score telling me to do that. You have to invent that kind of image anew each time you rehearse or perform. Only that kind of imagination can blow the dust off a two-hundred-year-old score, breathe life into it, and make it feel as bold and fresh as if it were the latest development on the evening news."

When the lunch was over I warmly thanked the maestro one final time. Then I took a slow walk back to the office. There was much to think about.

My mind kept returning to the scene he'd just described. I pictured it so vividly. There was this group of accomplished and dedicated singers doing their best, concentrating, applying all of their talent and training . . . yet in spite of it all their singing was stale.

Then the conductor said nine sentences that inspired life, energy, motivation, and determination in the chorus. They suddenly rededicated themselves not only to the task at hand, but to a higher purpose that lifted every note and syllable that they sang.

He changed the very meaning of who the singers were and what they were doing. They weren't just some group practicing in some rehearsal studio sometime in the early twenty-first century. They represented an entire people at a defining moment in their history, raising their voices on behalf of generations past and future.

It took me quite a few minutes before I realized why this before-and-after scene was stuck in my mind. The before was like my company as I had found it, when I first took the job. Many people were rowing hard, but our ship was still dangerously adrift. The after was like what the company might become with the right kind of leadership at the helm.

When my people arrive at work every day they're probably concerned with whatever final deadlines they're up against, wondering how they'll get through their in-box between all the meetings they're expected to attend. They're caught up in their personal to-do lists and, like the chorus, they may well be stuck in a routine that supports the status quo.

What if their leaders produced a unifying vision for the future that they and everyone around them could embrace? A vision so deeply grounded in the company's mission that it redefined for everybody what the work was about. The pursuit of this overarching vision would lift people's awareness beyond their day-to-day concerns to a discovery of new possibilities that become suddenly and brilliantly visible. What might we be like if I could inspire my people to invest in a future like that?

I was so lost in thought during my walk that, before I knew it, I had arrived at my building. But instead of going back to the office I made a beeline for our library, in search of an Italian–English dictionary. I quickly thumbed through it until I found the entry I was looking for.

Maestro was defined as a master, teacher, tutor, or instructor. I felt somehow unsatisfied, as if there was something important that these definitions didn't reveal. So I made my way to the office of a colleague who was born and raised in Italy. He listened with friendly eyes as I asked for a deeper understanding of what the word meant to an Italian.

"Well," he replied, "of course the dictionary is right. *Maestro* can mean all of these things. But to me it's always meant 'teacher,' with an important, subtle distinction. The maestro is not the one who teaches you all the facts that you need for your diploma, or trains you in your specialty. No," he said, shaking his head, "that is the *professore*.

"The maestro is the one who lays the foundation for learning, who teaches the principles and the values: the curiosity about the world, the confidence that education eventually leads to freedom, the courage to strive for something higher than just satisfying your appetite, the ideals that last throughout your life. That is the maestro."

I thanked him and walked through the corridors toward my office. There was a lot of work to be done.

Acknowledgments

While the events of this story are the product of my imagination they are all based on actual experience. I have repeatedly sought the counsel of business executives who had engaged me to present Music Paradigm sessions to their organizations. Every scene depicted in these pages did in fact happen. In constructing the story I've selected those problems and solutions that came up repeatedly in many diverse organizations. I am therefore indebted to the hundreds of executives, consultants and coaches with whom I've had the privilege of collaborating. Some of them deserve special mention for the important role they've played in shaping this book.

Paul Kahn was the brilliant visionary who could see the potential value of The Music Paradigm when it was barely a figment of my imagination. He showed me how to turn a possibility into a reality. Stuart Blinder was the remarkable business strategist and innovator whose outstanding success leading the supply chain of Lever Brothers inspired so much of this book. Sheldon Czapnik helped me turn a mountain of anecdotal data into a structured story, and prevented me from going down countless blind alleys. Ed Stanford gave me confidence that the holistic experiential learning of The Music Paradigm could be translated into a book, and infallibly offered sage advice about which challenge to take up next. When I needed a deeper insight or clearer understanding about a particular business issue I would frequently turn to Neville Osrin, Ulrich Nettesheim, Steve Kirn or Ken Kesslin. Their fingerprints can be found everywhere in these pages.

This being my first book, I had no idea that a great publisher could make such a dramatic difference. Adrian Zackheim had the imagination to see what my manuscript draft could become, once he helped me clarify the central ideas, streamline the narrative and drive it forward. Adrienne Schultz helped make every page of the text so much more readable. Will Weisser and Maureen Cole along with Elizabeth Hayes showed me how bringing the book into the public arena could itself be a creative act.

Maestro would never have been possible without the experience of delivering hundreds of Music Paradigm sessions to organizations throughout the entire world. In each case there were inspired leaders who believed that great music could add enormous value to a business meeting and took the risk of enrolling their companies in the plan. I know that many put their reputations and careers on the line by strongly advocating for such an out-of-the-box idea. This book is a tribute to them and to the success that they brought to their organizations.

In delivering live orchestral performance to so many meetings I relied on the dedicated support of the Music Paradigm staff. Each of them deserves mention: Myra Hess, Chris Thompson, Susan Spafford, Margot Johansen, Arlo McKinnon, John Ostrowski, Carol Rosenberg-McCool, Catherine Stewart-Lindley and Jan Thirlby.

For More Information

To learn more about Roger Nierenberg and The Music Paradigm, the unique experience that inspired this story, visit www.musicparadigm.com

The Music Paradigm is a highly flexible, high-impact learning experience that works equally well for groups as small as 25 or as large as 2,000. Over the past decade hundreds of corporations, financial institutions, government agencies, law firms, not for profits, hospitals, universities, and community organizations around the world have sponsored Music Paradigm sessions for their people. The session provides a memorable group experience that generates fresh insights long after the meeting is over, and lessons that become part of the organization's dialogue and culture.

Are you interested in buying multiple copies of *Maestro* for your business, sales organization, school, non-profit, or house of worship? You can receive special discounted pricing, great service, direct shipping, and more through Penguin's Business-to-Business advantage program. The program allows your local bookstore to offer special discounted pricing on this book for bulk sales. Call your local bookstore and say you'd like to use Penguin's B2B program to buy copies of *Maestro* for giveaway or training.

_____ *Maestro* 978-1-59184-288-0 $19.95 ($25.00 CAN)